KEEP IT
SIMPLE

KEEP IT
SIMPLE

DANIEL J. HAIGHT

Newberry, FL 32669

Bridge-Logos, Inc.
Newberry, FL 32669

Keep It Simple
Eight Truths that Transform Life, Business and Relationships
by Daniel J. Haight

Printed in the United States of America.

Library of Congress Catalog Card Number: 2018931858

International Standard Book Number: 978-1-61036-470-6

DEDICATION

Writing a book takes a lot of dedicated people. Thank you Arlene Moskwa who has always taken the time to take my long hand and translate it into something legible. I've had a lot of help over the years. No one has helped me more than my wife of over 30 years, Joselyn. She's the love of my life and greatest helper a man could have. Thank you Joselyn.

FOREWORD

We all want to succeed and to have a life of meaning and purpose. Sometimes we just need a place to begin. In this book, *Keep It Simple*, my friend Daniel Haight provides that starting point. With great wisdom and captivating personal experiences, Daniel presents solid life principles which will lead to unparalleled success and purpose if you take this knowledge and apply it in your life. You need both the knowledge and the sweat equity that is required to put these principles into practice. There is no better time than right now to read this book, internalize its concepts, and make them part of your daily routine. You will never regret making yourself better, and you will be uniquely rewarded as you see the impact of your achievement becoming visible in the people around you.

—**DR. DAVE MARTIN**, YOUR SUCCESS COACH, AND
AUTHOR OF *THE 12 TRAITS OF THE GREATS*

ACKNOWLEDGMENTS

Thank you, Charles.

ENDORSEMENTS

Keep It Simple is a gold mine of wisdom nuggets and truths learned from many years of experience. Danny destroys the myth that success and a meaningful life is a secret or complicated. If you want a self-help book that will help you suffer in comfort, this book is not for you! But if you want a transformation in your life, marriage, and business, *Keep It Simple* offers you and rocket-ride out of the mediocre!

—**RICK GODWIN**, PASTOR AND FOUNDER OF SUMMIT CHRISTIAN CENTER, SAN ANTONIO, TX

As America's #1 Wealth Coach, I would confidently recommend that you add *Keep It Simple* Somebody by Pastor Daniel Haight to your personal self-empowerment library! These pragmatic and practical teachings are insightful and uncomplicated. This simple approach to one's choice to be successful is "right on the money!"

—**DR. MICHAEL CHITWOOD**, PROFESSIONAL SPEAKER, AUTHOR OF RICH GOD, POOR GOD, WEALTH AND FINANCE EXPERT, PRESIDENT/CEO OF MICHAEL CHITWOOD INTERNATIONAL

In a world impressed with complexity and give to overthinking issues, *Keep It Simple* reminds us you don't have to. Pastor Daniel Haight reminds us that simple is not being simplistic and simplifying is the key to a successful life.

—**SAM CHAND**, LEADERSHIP CONSULTANT AND AUTHOR OF BIGGER FASTER LEADERSHIP

Years ago someone told me that often the word "Theology" was the art of making the simple things of God hard. In *Keep It Simple*, Pastor Danny from many years of experience presents simple steps to achieving major goals in your life! God has made His plan simple and we have made it hard. In this book Pastor Danny presents simple truths to help us fulfill our destiny!

—**DR. DAVID T. DEMOLA**, PASTOR EMERITUS AND FOUNDER OF FAITH FELLOWSHIP MINISTRIES WORLD OUTREACH CENTER IN SAYREVILLE, NJ (DECEASED)

In his newest book, Daniel Haight provides us all with a rich resource of inspiration, motivation, and wisdom for the practical everyday issues each one of us face. Dan has an amazing way of mixing metaphor, humor, and straightforward life principles that everyone can apply. May the truths in this book find a home in your heart and further you down the path of realizing your hopes and dreams.

—**JOHN WAGNER**, PASTOR FAITH FELLOWSHIP MINISTRIES WORLD OUTREACH CENTER, SAYREVILLE, NJ

When Jesus tells us in Matthew 6:33 to seek first the Kingdom of God, His purpose wasn't to just give us a series of do's and don'ts in life. God's kingdom principles are the secret to a life of fulfillment, purpose, success and prosperity. I have known Pastor Danny for over 30 years and I believe that he has been given an ability by the Holy Spirit to make these Kingdom Principles simple, understandable and easy to apply to our everyday lives. If we will receive what Pastor Danny reveals to us in his book and apply these principles to our everyday lives, we will become exactly what God has designed all of us to become: prosperous, happy and guiding lights to a generation so desperately in need of successful role models.

—**JAMES PETROW**, PASTOR AND FOUNDER OF HOUSE ON THE ROCK, WINDGAP, PA

My friend Danny is the somebody who has kept it simple! This book is so easy to read and understand. Many books have been written about success and "how to" manuals, but very few are this practical. The wisdom and simplicity of application in this book makes it truly help others find their way. Danny, I hope we all "Keep It Simple."

—**JOE MCKELVEY**, PASTOR AND FOUNDER OF CHRISTIAN FAITH FELLOWSHIP INC., MIDDLETOWN, NY

Tune your ears to the word of wisdom; set your heart on a life of understanding (Proverbs 2:2MSG) In his book *Keep It Simple* Pastor Daniel Haight shares sound principles that you can instantly apply to every area of life. He delivers simplified strategies that will empower you to achieve greater success. You will discover that having the right information doesn't have to be complicated, it actually can be simple.

—**JOHN ANTONUCCI**, PASTOR OF THE FAITH CENTER, FORT MYERS, FL

Pastor Daniel Haight's book *Keep It Simple* brings together 8 practical truths that are simple to apply and yet life changing. In each of these truths we see how it's the simple little things that can get us moving forward. I highly recommend this book if you're looking to grown into all that God has for you in life.

—**TOM FEOLA**, PASTOR OF CHRISTIAN FAITH FELLOWSHIP CHURCH, HARDYSTON, NJ

I have known Dan Haight for over 25 years. He is a passionate communicator that connects to his audience through practical life-changing truths. As you read these pages, prepare to plug these precepts into every area of your life today!

—**FRED MCCARTHY**, LEAD PASTOR OASIS CHRISTIAN CENTER, RAHWAY, NJ

Pastor Danny is able to make things so simple, practical, and relevant. This is a quick and easy read that will serve as a reminder of what will make our lives and the lives of others better as we put into practice what we glean from *Keep It Simple!*

—**RON CORZINE**, PRESIDENT, CHRISTIAN FELLOWSHIP INTERNATION

This book, *Keep It Simple* is a precious guide full of important principles of wisdom and truth written with heart. It can benefit those of us who want to improve our perspective in life, business and relationships. It is written by a Pastor who is a true sincere friend.

—**MICHAEL D'ANNA**, PRESIDENT OF GOSPEL FORUM, ITALY

Sometimes the truth is hard to embrace. But, when embraced, you will be propelled into flight; you will be able to *"soar high on wings like eagles," "run and not grow weary," "walk and not faint."* (Isaiah 10:31 NLT) Pastor Daniel has tapped into "truth" that has enlightened me (the reader) with wisdom that brings simple answers to complex questions. I'm confident that others who read this book will also identify, be enlightened and propelled into flight!

—**ARTHUR HALLETT**, NATIONAL DIRECTOR, EVANGELISM EXPLOSION
INTERNATIONAL PRISON MINISTRIES

Daniel J. Haight masterfully proves profundity can be found in simplicity. *Keep It Simple* is incredibly insightful and positively practical. It is a great read—enlightening, encouraging and enriching.

—**DR. LAWRENCE POWELL**, SENIOR PASTOR OF AGAPE FAMILY
WORSHIP CENTER, RAHWAY, NJ

TABLE OF CONTENTS

INTRODUCTION

Many years ago, when I was working as an associate Pastor at a very large religious organization, I was assigned to travel to a beautiful Caribbean country for two weeks. I was part of a leadership team doing some front work for a missions outreach with a vision to reach the poor and desperate in that country with supplies, food, literature and the good news of the Gospel. Our mission was simple, meet with our contacts in that country, build a rapport with the locals, speak at several churches and groups. We also were to set up some radio interviews and meet with participating pastors to build a stage for a crusade that would be the culmination of the two-week mission.

Our main contact was a very influential man in this country. He was the former Governor of the country, which is like our President here in the States. He was a multi- millionaire and religious leader who was familiar to almost everyone on the island. He couldn't have been more valuable and helpful to us as he streamlined the permitting process, equipment rentals and introduction to the who's who of the country. He even invited us to use one of the parks he owned to have our crusade in.

During those two weeks, he and I hit it off and we were able to spend a great deal of time together. I learned so much from him in those two weeks. The insight and education I gained was incredible. As a matter of fact, the time I spent with him was transformative. I learned first hand that success is as much caught as taught. Just being in his presence was a crash course on time management, delegation and vision. No question it was an education in life, business and ethics. In particular, I learned firsthand that you don't need everybody to like you to get a big job done, you just need the right people to like you.

* * * *

YOU DON'T NEED EVERYONE TO LIKE YOU TO GET A JOB DONE JUST THE RIGHT PEOPLE!

* * * *

He had many businesses and tremendous wealth. I was intrigued by his notoriety and asked him about his success. "I see your name on many buildings and businesses," I said. "Wherever I go with you, people know who you are and ask you to do things for them. You have car dealerships, jewelry stores, restaurants, parks, real estate and apartment complexes."

I went on to ask, "How did you do this? Did you inherit it all?"

He simply smiled as he answered, "Oh no, I didn't inherit anything. I was an orphan child here in this country. I had no father or mother to point me in the right direction in life. I had no one to give me money or assets for the future. I started with nothing. In fact, I did it the old fashion way, I learned it and I earned it!"

He took a few minutes and told me that even as a young boy he became desperate not to live in poverty or lack. He said being desperate, destitute and ignorant keeps you on a track to nowhere. I heard him loud and clear. Being poor, desperate and lonely was a choice! I decided even then not to be a victim. He said failures are really good at making excuses. He said with God's help I can win in life. My friend said boldly I could have excuses or have results but I couldn't have both! I recalled him quoting Matthew 6:33, *"But seek first the kingdom of God and His righteousness, and all these things shall be added to you."*

BEING DESPERATE KEEPS YOU ON A TRACK TO NOWHERE!

I remembered that Moses sought God in Exodus 33:14, *"Now therefore, I pray, if I have found grace in Your sight, show me now Your way, that I may know You and that I may find grace in Your sight..."*

This pillar of the community went on to talk about his struggles as a young orphaned boy walking barefoot over the small mountains that separated one half of the island from the other. He explained that there were times people would stop to give him a ride but most times he walked. He explained that he would dream of owning his own car, land, houses and businesses.

As he talked about his childhood and the obstacles he faced, I asked him, "How did you do all this and gain so much, including your political achievements?"

His answer was a breath of fresh air. "I did two things consistently!" was his reply.

"Number one, I did the opposite of what poor people did."

He then reached into his desk drawer and took out a legal size paper with writing all over the front and back of the page. He made a color copy and handed it to me. He said memorize everything from front to back and if I did that, I would have the tools necessary to accomplish anything.

As he handed me a copy of his original, he said something that I realized even then was profound. I was in the presence of a man who had come from nothing to the highest political office of his country. He was an orphaned boy who must have started with every insecurity, excuse and dysfunction that any poverty stricken child would have. Yet he amassed a fortune, literally millions in businesses, real estate and political success by simply doing the opposite of what the typical poor person does.

His second key was, "Keep it simple!"

KEEP IT SIMPLE!

When I asked him what that meant, he said, "Don't complicate the uncomplicated."

He went on to explain, "Success and failure are both choices. They're what you do every day. Success and failure are a matter of choice not chance. Every minor and major decision you make in life has consequences and repercussions."

As I looked at the paper he handed me, I saw famous quotes, quips, sayings and scriptures all over the page. He then boldly said, "This is the way I live my life!"

He told me to take responsibility for my life, have a goal for my future, faith, family, finances and friends. He also encouraged me to put first things first from God's viewpoint and to always forgive others while expecting God's favor in everything. He said even though it may not seem like much, make progress each day. He said, "I guess the biggest thing I did was I made up my mind I wouldn't quit". After each meeting with this dynamic man, I would go back to my hotel and ponder these life lessons. I made notes because I knew this was a life changing encounter that might never come my way again. I put a huge value on this opportunity because I know God could have given it to others.

As I started writing this book I asked myself, "Really? Another self-help book?" I know that there are a myriad of self-help books on the market today and I wondered, why produce another? Is there room for one that's basic and user friendly and results driven?

I believe that in many cases the blind have been leading the blind. Many self-help books don't keep it simple at all but the very opposite. Keeping it simple means the steps to reversing failure are as easy as action, attitude and the correct information. I've spoken to over four thousand different audiences and congregations over the last 28 years, ranging from twenty people in a classroom or a cell groups, to thousands in large auditoriums. I've spoken to athletes, actors, accountants, astronauts and executives; to the mega rich and famous as well as the desperately poor and obscure. I've learned that we all have a few things in common.

- We all have twenty-four hours in a day.
- We all use those hours differently.
- John Maxwell has said that if he could follow us around for just one day, he could predict our future.
- We have dreams and goals, no matter how old or young we are and that we hope will come to pass somehow.
- Everyone gets to a place in their life when they throw their hands up. They realize they've hit a wall and need help..

That is why I have written this book, because people need help. Too many have attended success seminars conducted by gurus and experts who aren't successful themselves. We even have TV Evangelists teaching others how to live victorious lives who are getting divorces and are in and out of scandals. I've even paid hundreds of dollars to attend seminars that once I left the meetings I knew had not gotten my money's worth. They were led by charismatic teachers and great motivational speakers but they themselves had little life experience and no process so attenders could realize functional change. There's actually a seminar out there right now that teaches you how to fake it till you make it in life and business.

I find it hard to understand why anyone would attend a seminar on success that is led by people who are not successful. The "fake it till you make it," and "win at any cost," mentality has permeated the church world. My father used to say, "Don't tell me how to make teepees until you've walked in my moccasins." Many years ago I heard it said that if it isn't working at home, don't export it.

I heard a story about a second grade teacher who asked her students to write a short essay about either their mom or dad. One little boy wrote that his dad can climb the highest mountain, can fly the fastest jet, can beat the meanest tiger but most of the time he just takes out the garbage. Even a second grader could see that his dad wasn't fulfilling his potential and had gotten stuck in the ruts of his life.

I trust that the words in the upcoming chapters will ignite not only motivation but a process of change in your lives. You are not down and out nor enjoying your last hoorah. You are not a lost cause or a casualty in life's lottery. If you are a believer in God, your playing field has unlimited potential no matter what the circumstance. It doesn't matter if you are facing a lion, a dungeon, a giant with only a slingshot or a stack of bills and bankruptcy. You have a God who loves you and wants to help you overcome anything and everything. In fact, the problem is not your problem, it's what you think about the problem that is the problem.

"Behold, I give you the authority to trample on serpents and scorpions, and over all the power of the enemy, and nothing shall by any means hurt you." —Luke 10:19

Remember, the early believers turned the world upside down for God. Although they faced great opposition, they didn't let the start stop them!

Let's keep it simple and trust God with the future. Here are eight pragmatic and practical principles that will help you out of any mess you are currently in and help you make progress. Once you grasp the message, be sure to share it with others. It's impossible to help someone else without helping yourself. The Keep It Simple mentality is don't let the start stop you!

START WHERE YOU ARE. DON'T LET THE START STOP YOU!

"Winning starts with Beginning." —Robert Schuller

Facing the fact that our choices have gotten us to where we are, that is a hard pill to swallow. You may be in a tight spot but your power of choice changes everything. Give yourself a break and stop condemning yourself for not being where you want to be. Right choices will determine the next chapter of your life so make them count! My beginning to changing my mindset was when I pressed my new friend about how he had accumulated all his wealth and influence.

He said, "I kept things very simple. Instead of lamenting over being an orphan and having very few assets, contacts, knowledge and experience, I just started where I was. There was nowhere else to go but up!"

There's really no cutting corners to anywhere worth going. Dubious short cuts are for the chumps and slicksters. Never confuse your soul with toxic information, what you don't have or the lack of resources that others may have that you don't. Let's look at the space shuttle program for example. Each time they blasted off from Cape Canaveral or Cape Kennedy, we see two or three large fuel cells attached to the outside of the shuttle. Just a few minutes after takeoff, those big fuel cells dropped off the shuttle because once in outer space there's little gravitational pull. There is no more need for the large fuel tanks for take off. It always takes extra energy and effort to get any project, business or endeavor off the ground. Stop carrying extra emotional baggage around that does nothing but hinder you. Why this and how come that? Why did others get the breaks? Stop all that useless talk. It's weighing you down. The journey you're on will be trying enough without all the extra self-inflicted mental junk.

In fact, we all are going to face challenges as we get started. There will always be a lack of resources, lack of contacts, lack of inventory or a less than perfect location or conditions to deal with. We will usually face some sort of discouragement either from family, friends or our competition. It is important to remember not to lose focus on the dream as you are getting started. Be ready to give that extra push and dig deep within for the extra energy needed to get off the launch pad and away from the gravitational pull of starting. Chase your dream with abandon! Keep in mind one real hindrance to success is chasing two different dreams at the same time.

CHASE YOUR DREAM WITH ABANDON!

This orphaned boy did not get bogged down by what he didn't have. He didn't allow his lack of education, experience, assets or opportunity stop his dream. Using his journey as an example, it is important to start where you are, keep it simple and inventory what you do have.

There was one of the true keys to my friend's success in life. It was his SELF TALK. What you say to yourself you truly believe because you've probably repeated it to yourself over and over in your thinking.

We will talk about this more in depth in a later chapter, but your self-talk is powerful! This abandoned orphan boy got past the natural negative self-talk of "nobody loves me," "my parents abandoned me," "I'm all alone in the world," "I have no future." He got past all that by realizing each good decision would be a building block for a better life.

Someone said you can have excuses, or you can have results, but you can't have both. Self-talk either offers a better life and encouragement that there's a better life waiting out there, or it can paralyze you into mediocrity and pessimism. You can choose your self talk like you choose the radio station in your car. He did it the same way we all must do! There are no shortcuts. We program our thinking with positive, scriptural conversations in our minds. That is why meditating the Word is so important. Meditation is not a bad thing, it simply means continued, or extended thought, reflection, contemplation. That is how we program our thinking.

Proverbs 23:7 AMP states that "as he (a man or woman) thinks in his heart, so is he." Control your self talk, and you control your future. It's a simple as that. Repetition is the key to self talk as it is content. The bible gives us the greatest self talk template there is. If you catch yourself thinking or talking negatively, say what God says about you: "because He who is in (me) you is greater than he (Satan) who is in the world" 1 John 4:4 AMP; "I can do all things through Christ Who strengthens me," Philippians 4:1 NKJV; "And God is able to make all grace [every favor and earthly blessing] come in abundance to (me) you, so that (I) you may always [under all circumstances, regardless of the need] have complete sufficiency in everything [being completely self-sufficient in Him], and have an abundance for every good work and act of charity." 2 Corinthians 9:8

AMP. There are literally thousands of positive confessions you can make from the Word of God. If you can change your thinking, you can change your direction in life.

I have written goals I carry in my wallet. Each time I open it I see them. I take a moment and glance at them daily and it affects my thinking and my self talk. My wife Joselyn says that those that say the can, and those that say they can't are both right. Declare war today against any self defeating thinking that comes into your mind. It's a trap that will keep you where you already are. Make the great exchange today in your thinking. Instead of saying "I should" say "I Will." Instead of saying "It's too late," say "I can do it." You make an imprint in your soul each time you turn a positive declaration from a negative one. Choose to believe you and God can do it. He's the Creator of this universe and He loves you! (John 3:16) The key is to get started changing old thinking patterns. It's not easy but then again it's not impossible. As a matter of fact, it's not only possible it's promised if you renew your mind according to Romans 12:1-2, which urges us to be transformed by renewing our minds to the Word of God. Encourage yourself hourly if you must, that if that little boy, broke and afraid, abandoned and neglected did so much to overcome and change his destiny, you can also. You and God can do it. Take pen and paper and write for yourself a daily confession of your goals and desires. Confess your trust in God's ability and power for your life and future. Start your day on purpose and begin to challenge the status quo in your mind. No short cuts, no self pity! Nothing of substance was ever accomplished by a person dominated by a negative mentality. The young orphan boy knew there was nowhere else to go but up!

*   *   *   *

"IN THIS WORLD PAIN IS INEVITABLE,
BUT SUFFERING IS OPTIONAL."

*   *   *   *

Take the first step. More information and assets will come as you go! God is faithful. You'll be amazed how God will bring people and opportunity as you blast off. Depression or regret are the biggest waste of time. Getting started with a real vision for your life is what's going to make up for lost time.

I have several businesses, most of which I started with very little. I've learned not to complicate my life with the fact that I did not have optimal resources to get started. Keep this in mind as you begin your next venture.

King David did not have a sword when he took off after the giant to cut off his head.

"Then David said to the Philistine, 'You come to me with a sword, with a spear, and with a javelin. But I come to you in the name of the Lord of hosts, the God of the armies of Israel, whom you have defied. This day the Lord will deliver you into my hand, and I will strike you and take your head from you. And this day I will give the carcasses of the camp of the Philistines to the birds of the air and the wild beasts of the earth, that all the earth may know that there is a God in Israel. Then all this assembly shall know that the Lord does not save with sword and spear; for the battle is the Lord's, and He will give you into our hands.'

So it was, when the Philistine arose and came and drew near to meet David, that David hurried and ran toward the army to meet the Philistine." —1 Samuel 17:45-48

Much of what you will need to further your project will be supplied as you go. Information and resources will be accumulated as you blast off through study and networking. Whether it is through trial and error or wisdom from others, you will get a great education as you take the steps toward your future.

I always keep it simple when it comes to information and assets. I'm not shy about asking others who are ahead of me what steps they would take in my circumstances. I've helped many folks get into the same businesses I'm in. One of the keys to success in life is to help others around you get to a better level in their lives. You never want to arrive at success alone. When you get right down to it, there is nothing quite as rewarding as helping others who need help.

YOU NEVER WANT TO ARRIVE AT SUCCESS ALONE!

You can't be shy when it comes to asking for help. James 4:2(b), *"Yet you do not have because you do not ask."* That scripture makes it pretty plain. If you never ask for help, then you already have your no. Most people like to help and it costs nothing to take the chance by asking others for advice, help and influence.

> *"Ask, and it will be given to you; seek, and you will find; knock, and it will be opened to you."* —Matthew 7:7

Ronald Reagan, former President of the United States, said, "We can't help everyone, but everyone can help someone." There is help out there for you and your future. Brian Tracy, author and successful businessman, said, "Successful people are always looking for opportunities to help others. Unsuccessful people are always asking 'What's in it for me?'"

Truly successful people want to help others, so ask for it. Keep it simple and don't flood your life with a bunch of excuses. When we get right down to the nitty gritty, we all need help breaking barriers in life. This man went from being an orphan child walking over mountains barefoot, be the Governor of the country and a multimillionaire. That simply tells me that he had a lot of help and no give in, give up or give out.

The only thing stopping you from going from where you are to where you want to be, is information and the guts to believe it is possible for you to get there. God will provide you with the help you need. There are no two ways about it. It takes good old fashioned guts to change your life. It takes courage to chase a dream, pursue a goal or start a business. Oftentimes you have to become your own biggest cheerleader because there will be more doubters than believers.

IT TAKES COURAGE TO CHASE A DREAM!

It takes others to help us grow beyond our present environment. That is where most people get stuck. They never leave their hometowns or go on exciting vacations because they are stuck in the "I've always done it this way" environment. They are like the baby shark that has the potential of growing to seven or eight feet in length but, in an eight-foot aquarium, never grows beyond ten inches. Take that same shark and take him out of the eight-foot aquarium and set him free to grow in the Atlantic Ocean and he will grow to upwards of eight feet in length.

Roger Bannister and all the other milers of his day were told it was physically impossible to ever break the four-minute mile. That is until he did it and then dozens went on to break it over the next year and a half. We all need help getting out of our small thinking.

Les Brown, the great motivational speaker, said, "Help others achieve their dreams and you will achieve yours." So, the quickest way I know of to change any environment is to ask someone who is where you want to be to help you get there. Don't expect them to do it for you because they won't. They're busy doing their own work.

The orphan boy asked for help and got it all the way to the Governor's office.

Many people wait for that one big moment in life to be discovered and don't realize that each day is a big moment that prepares you for the next big opportunity. Someone once said big things are hiding inside little things waiting to be discovered and only the diligent realize it. I recently heard about a woman just starting in the movie business in New York City. She had a chance to meet and network with someone she deemed to be a small time player in the film industry. Because of her perceptions, she felt it would be a waste of time to meet with someone she considered, "small potatoes." I believe that she was making a colossal mistake to miss out on an opportunity to get to know anyone in the industry. Everybody knows something or someone we don't know. That person might have known someone that might have been key to her future. Big doors open on small hinges Hurricane Carter, a middleweight boxer in the 1960's, once said, "I think many times God watches us when we deal with 'small potatoes,' before He graduates us to our next phase in life."

BIG DOORS OPEN ON SMALL HINGES!

"But David said to Saul, 'Your servant used to keep his father's sheep, and when a lion or a bear came and took a lamb out of the flock, I went out after it and struck it, and delivered the lamb from its mouth; and when it arose against me, I caught it by its beard, and struck and killed it. Your servant has killed both lion and bear; and this uncircumcised Philistine will be like one of them, seeing he has defied the armies of the living God.'" —1 Samuel 17:34-36

David faced a lion and a bear before he ever faced Goliath. I believe his greatest battle was keeping his heart right while dealing with Saul's dysfunction and jealousy. Doing the little things is a big deal!

"But David said to Abishai, 'Do not destroy him; for who can stretch out his hand against the Lord's anointed, and be guiltless?' David said furthermore, 'As the Lord lives, the Lord shall strike him, or his day shall come to die, or he shall go

*out to battle and perish. The Lord forbid that I should stretch
out my hand against the Lord's anointed.'"*

—1 Samuel 26:9-11

Another key after getting started is choose to become a lifelong learner. Your environment should always improve! There's no short cut to anywhere worth going. Learn your craft and then learn some more. David learned he wasn't fighting alone.

BE A LIFE LONG LEARNER!

Most of David's contemporaries would have run away from a "mano a mano" face off with Goliath. But, not David!

*"Moreover David said, 'The Lord, who delivered me from the
paw of the lion and from the paw of the bear, He will deliver
me from the hand of this Philistine.' And Saul said to David,
'Go, and the Lord be with you!'"*   —1 Samuel 17:37

David learned where his strength came from.

One of the keys to David's victories over his circumstances was not to wait until he needed help before asking for it. In other words, David didn't know there would be giants in his future yet he started preparing to change his environment years before he needed the help.

*"And Samuel said to Jesse, 'Are all the young men here?'
Then he said, 'There remains yet the youngest, and there he
is, keeping the sheep.' And Samuel said to Jesse, 'Send and
bring him. For we will not sit down till he comes here.' So
he sent and brought him in. Now he was ruddy, with bright
eyes, and good-looking. And the Lord said, 'Arise, anoint him;
for this is the one!' Then Samuel took the horn of oil and
anointed him in the midst of his brothers; and the Spirit of
the Lord came upon David from that day forward. So Samuel
arose and went to Ramah."*   —1 Samuel 16:11-13

David spent years in the fields caring for and protecting the family's flocks. He was busy honing his craft in obscurity. While everyone who meant anything to him was discounting him and his future, David was practicing with his sling while the sheep were grazing. He didn't wait until there was a nine foot nine-inch giant in front of him to prepare. David was a slinger.

> *"Among all this people were seven hundred select men who were left-handed; every one could sling a stone at a hair's breadth and not miss."* —Judges 20:16

He was among a group of highly trained and revered marksmen who used a sling and and smooth stones in battles.

Start where you are. David prepared himself in the field, hour after hour; when no one was looking but God. He was relentless in his preparation. In Malcolm Gladwell's book, David and Goliath, it goes into great detail about David's training environment. If you wait to prepare, prepare to wait!

● ● ● ●

IF YOU WAIT TO PREPARE, PREPARE TO WAIT!

● ● ● ●

Whatever your field of study or desired profession, get busy learning and developing for your future. Figure out what you want to do and start your journey. They say it takes about 10 years to become an overnight success. I love what Dr. Michael Chitwood says. "If you want something you've never had you must to do something you've never done." Maybe you don't really know what you want to do yet. Begin by asking yourself the tough questions. Questions like, 'What am I good at?' 'What do others think I'm good at?' 'What have I excelled at in the past?' 'What do I get excited about?' 'What keeps my interest?' Then, look around at your own environment. What books are on your shelf and is there a theme that you seem to keep repeating in those books?

If a small orphan boy can do it, so can you!

FOCUS!

So, just get started and don't wait for the perfect conditions. Ask others for help and be patient. It's going to take many years to be an overnight success. You could take some online classes to see if there is a genuine interest in an area. Passion is a real ingredient your future and you shouldn't have to manufacture zeal for your destiny. Dale Carnegie said, "People rarely succeed unless they have fun in what they are doing."

For me it was simple. I just did what I had to do. I wasn't qualified to do it nor was I educated to enter into the field. I had no contacts or degrees, but I didn't let that be a barrier to my passion. I got educated. Every waking moment was an opportunity to learn. I devoured books, attended teaching seminars and I changed my education environment. Was it easy? I had to contend with dyslexia, so of course it was quite a challenge. I had never spoken in public for more than twenty to thirty seconds during interviews after sporting events in high school. I simply did what I had to do. Talent is overrated in most cases. I know plenty of talented people that never made it off the launching pad of life.

I believe that excuses are crutches used by the uncommitted; so become committed if you want to succeed. You can keep it simple and not overcomplicate things. I have a friend who has now passed on. His name was David and he was one of the good guys in life. I remember a story he told when he was drafted during the Vietnam War. They noticed that he was a musician from his paperwork and the sergeant asked him what instrument he played. David told him the saxophone. The sergeant told him that he needed a flute player and asked David if he could learn the flute in two weeks. David said yes and the sergeant then told him that if he couldn't, David would be put into the infantry. Not only did David learn the flute, he became really proficient in the two weeks because he was committed and obviously motivated.

How bad do you want your future? Maybe that is the best place to be in life. Not what do I want to do? But what do I have to do with my life? It will be a monumental moment in time when you realize and declare your decision about the direction of your life! At that point, you need to declare it from the mountaintop that you have figured it out!

THE BEST PLACE TO BE IS NOT WHAT DO I WANT TO DO? BUT WHAT DO I HAVE TO DO WITH MY LIFE

My wife figured out her path rather easily. She also did what she had to do to bring her future into her present. In her early 20's, she was going through life working, clubbing and partying. At a club one night, a girl witnessed to her about giving her heart to Christ. She knew she had to get out of there or she would have to make some serious changes in her life. Instead of changing she told the girl God is for the weak. What do I need Him for? Within a year she met a young lady who had traveled from California to share the Gospel and hand out evangelism tracts in NYC. That changed my wife's life for eternity. It took about a year but Joselyn learned God isn't for the weak, but for the lost. Once Joselyn got saved she knew she to had to use her life to help others. Joselyn has been singing in churches and conferences, preaching and going on mission trips for 30 years now. It began when she just did what she had to do.

She learned to play the guitar and piano and began to write music. Today she has recorded two CD's that are being enjoyed by many all over the world. She knew that she had to pursue music. What is it that you have to pursue? There is the 5000 hour rule that says if you can invest 5000 hours into something, you can become an expert. Passion and desire can make up for a lot of those hours but hard work and knowledge are the key. In fact, you don't have to be an expert to begin.

For some, looking at your mentors can be intimidating, even depressing because of how easy they make it look. Just start out by becoming proficient while growing and allow your gifting to propel you through the start up phase into becoming an expert.

ALLOW YOUR GIFTING TO PROPEL YOU THROUGH THE START UP PHASE INTO BECOMING AN EXPERT!

The power triplets of getting started are: passion, gifting and opportunity. You are not in charge of any of those three, God is! You are just the manager. So don't let the start stop you. God has given you that inner fire and determination known as passion. He has gifted you with talent, courage and direction and it is He Who opens the doors that no one can shut. You are the custodian of the daily grind of God's gifts. You can both value what He has gifted you with and cooperate; or you can just hide and watch the parade go by. Millions of people remain frustrated with the status quo they tolerate everyday on their jobs. Choose to do what you have to do to make yourself fulfilled in life. Choose to follow your path with purpose and passion.

"Be diligent to present yourself approved to God, a worker who does not need to be ashamed, rightly dividing the word of truth." —2 Timothy 2:15

I've got some earth shattering news for you. The will of God is not automatic and God can't make you obey. There are some folks who have the idea that just because it's God's will for something to take place, it will happen regardless of their engagement or lack of it. That's a real cop out. That little orphan boy had to keep putting one foot in front of the other and pursue his dreams.

Here are a few keys to help in your decision making process, to follow your dream or to follow someone else.

- Inventory your talents
- Identify your passions
- Become unyielding in the face of pressure
- Determine to focus on development and growth in your field

In fact, your "I will" can dominate any obstacle you face as you blast off the launching pad. Remember, your mentors and the "professionals" didn't start off as they look now, twenty to thirty years later. Don't let the start stop you! You will be amazed at your development and the skills you acquire, activate and discover that were lying dormant within you.

DON'T LET THE START STOP YOU!

There are things I do today that I never saw years ago and probably would have intimidated me anyway. Since I got hold of these truths my possibilities grew and I have been on TV, radio, written books, magazine articles, spoken at conferences and seminars, served on boards and have been a recruiter and trainer, just to name a few. I'm sure your list will astound you too.

Unfortunately, the start stops many people. They either feel unqualified, intimidated by their mentors or wait for conditions to be perfect before they launch into the deep, probably the biggest hurdle we face.

It is important to be decisive and follow your dreams, talents and passions. The world always makes a place for passion and determination. God's favor will make up for any obstacle you face or deficiency you may encounter. Just decide today that you are going to make the choice to get started. Knowing what you want and launching toward it is half the battle. There may be some confusion during lift off but stay the course and, just like the orphan boy, you will make steady progress.

Let's explore some of the keys he used to get to where he wanted to go.

One of my brothers was small in stature. In this world, when you are small you are a natural target for bullies, especially when you have an older brother. When Mike was about fifteen, he woke up one day and decided that he wasn't going to be a victim of bullying anymore. He began to ride the bus three or four days a week to Karate classes several miles away. As his older brother, I paid little to no attention to his comings and goings as the weeks went by. Mike even tried to show all of us kids the things he was learning but we weren't really interested. It didn't take too long before he began to gain confidence and physically develop. Of course, his starting the process and his progress led to my not picking on him anymore and in fact, no one else did either.

Mike went to school, then class and then to his job. He had no one encouraging him nor did he have any aid from those around him as he began his journey. He pushed through many long and tiring days of school, Karate class and work with no fanfare or accolades. It took several years and he earned his black belt. Then he progressed further into it and applied more dedication and focus as his passion grew. He went on to study Krav Maga and Jiu Jitsu and actually won a gold medal at the Pan American Games in his age and weight class and became second in the world in the weight class above him. Mike went on to open a Karate School where hundreds of students learned confidence, fortitude, endurance, self-control and commitment. He was always dedicated to helping the bullied start their journey in Karate. In fact, many of his students went on to complete their black belts.

None of that would have happened for Mike or the hundreds of lives he changed if he had not started in what would have seemed an impossible environment. Don't allow the start to stop your dream! Simply dream out loud!

● ● ● ●

SIMPLY DREAM OUT LOUD!

● ● ● ●

"Now it came to pass after these things that God tested Abraham, and said to him, 'Abraham!' And he said, 'Here I am.' Then He said, 'Take now your son, your only son Isaac, whom you love, and go to the land of Moriah, and offer him there as a burnt offering on one of the mountains of which I shall tell you.'" —Genesis 22:1-2,

Abraham had partial information and that information probably did not foster confidence in God's leadership. The last thing Abraham wanted to do is set out on a trip without the knowledge of the final destination, nor did he want to sacrifice his son who had been a gift from God. Yet we see in Verse 3 that Abraham acted upon what he knew, *"So Abraham rose early in the morning and saddled his donkey, and took two of his young men with him, and Isaac his son; and he split the wood for the burnt offering, and arose and went to the place of which God had told him."*

The main point in this Verse is that you don't need to have complete knowledge to obey what you know is the voice and will of God. Abraham probably had as many questions as you and I would have had about the instructions but he rose up early and did what he knew to do. Whatever God does, He does it ethically, morally and consistently. So Abraham's trust of God was stronger than his need to understand the request to sacrifice his son. He knew God would explain as he went forward. We have to get to the place where we trust what we see in the Word of God more than what we see in the mirror. If we look in the mirror and see that our hair or make up is out of order, we trust the reflection and make adjustments.

For so many, there are things you know you were supposed to do but you didn't because you couldn't figure it all out. Maybe it didn't make sense at the time. Maybe you had more month than money and you talked yourself out of tithing. Or maybe you still felt pain so you gave up on your healing. Let me challenge you today. If Abraham obeyed in the face of everything contrary to logic and knowledge, you can also. The little orphan boy did.

> IF ABRAHAM OBEYED IN THE FACE OF EVERYTHING CONTRARY TO LOGIC AND KNOWLEDGE, YOU CAN ALSO.

Simply ask yourself if there is something you know you should be doing, even something that you believe God has led you to do, but you have stopped because you didn't understand or it really didn't make sense. You can obey with partial information. You can obey God and He will explain as you get further down the road of obedience. 1 Sam.15:22 *To obey is better than sacrifice*.

THE KEEP IT SIMPLE MENTALITY IS START WHERE YOU ARE!

2

DON'T DO WHAT THE UNSUCCESSFUL DO

I began to read the legal sized paper late at night before drifting off to sleep. Most of the comments, quips and sayings were familiar but some took me by surprise because of their simplicity. In the left margin there were bold letters that were underlined stating, "If you want to be successful, don't do what the unsuccessful do." So I began my own list. I started to search what unsuccessful people do and found about twenty common traits and habits. This partial list can help you locate yourself and others around you.

The unsuccessful:

- Waste time
- Stop learning
- Fear change
- Have no goals
- Blame others
- Hang around others who are unsuccessful
- Do what is convenient
- Give up in hard times
- Act emotionally
- Criticize achievers
- Make bad choices

These can be called habits, but your future will be determined by what you do or allow every day. You are already going to live out your days, so you might as well begin to break some bad habits and start new and improved ones that will bring you the future you desire. By merely exercising one hour a day and eating better, my wife and I lost a cumulative total of fifty pounds in a few months. We traded our bad habit of overeating and eating junk to proactively eating the right foods and starting a moderate exercising regime. It has been said that your future is hidden inside your daily routine.

YOUR FUTURE IS HIDDEN INSIDE YOUR DAILY ROUTINE!

As time went on, I was able to interview many people and I can tell you that these listed threads were noticeably common among the unsuccessful. Many had no vision beyond the weekend and no plan for their money, children or families. On average, there were many more who smoked, read much less, exercised less and had very high stress levels due to their bad choices than those who were successful. The actual studies done on this subject would rock your world.

Some of the simplest things like setting goals and having a direction in your life can make all the difference between success and failure and all that goes along with both. Merely making time to have family dinners at the table each night can change the entire dynamic of the family. Experts have seen that this simple adjustment of family dinners cuts the divorce rate considerably, and reduces teen suicide, drug use among teens and premarital sex by fifty per cent.

Making the choice to attend church as a family on a weekly basis, taking an active role in your children's homework assignments and talking around the table can be some of the most basic but important decisions that can help adolescents. Even praying together can be a very positive force in your children's lives.

There are some proven ways to help your children become successful and with the consistent application of these habits anyone can begin routines that will catapult them from mediocrity to success. As we saw in Verse 3, Abraham rose early and went where God wanted him to go. Going to bed at a decent hour and rising early can lay a wonderful foundation for the day. In fact, rising one hour early, before everyone gets up, gives you the opportunity to study, dream and plan which in turn can put a skip in your step and a song in your heart. It will also give you an extra 365 hours a year to think about your decisions, plan your day and make adjustments toward a more preferred future.

I've practiced this for years and believe that first hour can be the most important of each day. Whether you choose to exercise, dream or pray during that time, believe me, it is not wasted time but an investment in your future.

We can learn a lot from the simplicity of Verse 3.

- Abraham chose to obey even when he had limited information.
- He acted right away, before his circumstances would reason away his obedience.
- He knew God's character and that God would do the right things the right way.

Abraham rose early and went forth in what most would agree was an inconvenient and unconventional journey. There was a saying often used years ago about doing the inconvenient. "In this world of give and take, there are not enough people willing to give what it takes." Successful people do the inconvenient.

SUCCESSFUL PEOPLE DO THE INCONVENIENT!

Sadly, there are many people who have been stuck in neutral in life for months, years and even decades because they refuse to act on what they know. Unsuccessful people get nowhere in life because their history keeps repeating itself. There are mantras heard and repeated in their heads telling them they cannot do it or nothing good ever happens to them. They wonder why others get all the breaks and nobody will help them succeed or think that the entire world is against them.

It is time to make up your mind that you are going to do a self-examination and begin to cull out all the habits of the unsuccessful and rid your life of excuses.

Many years ago, I started asking myself questions like, 'who said I can't do it?" and "why not me?" I found out I was limiting and sabotaging my own future by practicing many of these negative habits.

That young orphan boy who started out with nothing, not only had to start where he was; but he also had to start with partial knowledge and information. Remember, the start stops many people and not knowing all the facts stops many others. You see, it is not what you don't know that is keeping you stuck, but it is what you know and refuse to act on.

* * * *

IT'S NOT WHAT YOU DON'T KNOW THAT IS KEEPING YOU STUCK, BUT IT IS WHAT YOU KNOW AND REFUSE TO ACT ON!

* * * *

Let's look again at Abraham in Verse 3, *"So Abraham rose early in the morning and saddled his donkey, and took two of his young men with him, and Isaac his son; and he split the wood for the burnt offering, and arose and went to the place of which God had told him."* Even with partial information and only a general direction to go, Abraham took off in total obedience.

This very successful businessman and politician didn't wait to begin until he had everything he needed. He already had his direction. Most times that is plenty of information and all you need to begin your journey. The real issues are which way do I want to go?, where do I want to end up?, and who do I want to become?

The road to your destination, whether it be education, health or financial prosperity, will start with a sign that will say, "Under Construction," because we all have work to do. It is important to disregard the "Dead End" signs and "U-Turn" signs along the way because you have a God who will help you with the impossibilities.

Always remember, God has more answers than we have questions, more wisdom than we have ignorance, and He has more provision than we have need!

The quicker you begin to ask yourself the tough questions in life the better.

Questions like, "Where do I want to be in a year or five years?" Questions like, "What will make me happy and what will pay the bills?" It is important to understand just how hard times and the unknown can disrupt your direction and resolve. Don't be detoured; don't do what the unsuccessful do.

As a young schoolboy, I was always the slow kid when it came to school work because there wasn't an understanding of dyslexia as there is today. Now schools can identify and help troubled children through the potholes and humiliation of dyslexia. In my day, they looked at me as dumb and slow. It was quite an awakening when I realized that I saw things differently and learned in a completely different way than your usual public school student. I had to memorize a lot more when it came to reading and English. I also continually transposed numbers, making math almost impossible.

Many of you are probably faced with things only you know about. The world has a way of pigeonholing all of us and isolating us, that small voice we all have that continually reminds us all the negative things about ourselves. In time, if unchecked, we start believing the lies we tell ourselves. If the devil or circumstances can keep us isolated then we are vulnerable to becoming unsuccessful or being an underachiever. I was convinced by not only my teachers and fellow students, but also by my self-talk, that I could never speak publicly or even read publicly.

Unsuccessful people stay in those traps of self-imposed limitations and never venture outside the safety of their controlled environment which has been set up to protect them from shame, fears or failure.

The orphan lad had a very long road ahead of him. People had abandoned him, neglected him and discounted him at every turn. It is at that point that God came in and changed his life forever. God comes into all our lives the same way as we see in Hebrews 13:5(b), *"For He Himself has said, 'I will never leave you nor forsake you.'"* God is a master at taking what people call junk and making something valuable out of it.

The great concert violinist Niccolò Paganini (1782-1840) was standing before a packed house, surrounded by a full orchestra. He was playing a number of difficult pieces, and he came to one of his favorites, which was a violin concerto.

Shortly after he was under way, one of the strings on his violin snapped and hung down from the instrument. Relying on his genius, he improvised and played on the next three strings. To his surprise (and the conductor's as well), a second string broke. Now there were two dangling strings as he again began to improvise and play the piece on the two remaining strings. You guessed it! Almost at the end of this magnificent concerto, a third string snapped. Now there were three dangling, and he finished the piece on one string.

The audience stood to their feet and applauded until their hands were numb. They never thought to ask for an encore; they expected to leave. But Paganini held his instrument high in the air and said, "Paganini and one string," and he proceeded to play an encore with the full orchestra.

He made more music from one string than many violinists ever could do on four.

The difference, of course, aside from his superb abilities, was one of attitude. Instead of falling into despair and self-pity, Paganini's splendid attitude allowed him to take a very difficult situation and turn it into a triumph.

Once you know what direction you need to go in order to start your journey, don't wait for the perfect conditions or you'll be waiting a long time. Ecclesiastes 11:4 (Amp), *"He who watches the wind [waiting for all conditions to be perfect] will not sow [seed], and he who looks at the clouds will not reap [a harvest]."*

DON'T WAIT FOR THE PERFECT CONDITIONS OR YOU'LL BE WAITING A LONG TIME!

Abraham got the servants, donkeys and split wood and set off toward Moriah with not much to go on; but what he had was enough. If God is talking to you about being a missionary, I'd start by getting a passport. You may not even know where to travel and serve yet and have not yet raised a single dollar for support, but you can get a passport.

I attended Bible School after my conversion. I did not ever know if it was the right school but I got started. Keep in mind a car that is not moving is hard to steer! I packed a little red Pinto station wagon which was given to me by my older brother Dennis and drove all night to Tulsa Oklahoma. Believe me when I tell you that conditions in my life were not perfect. In fact, they would have had to improve by a very long way to even get to where you could see the light at the end of the tunnel. But that is where I was and that is where I began.

I'll never forget the words written on the legal pad in bold capitals, "Don't Do What the Unsuccessful Do!" Once I read that, I started making mental notes of the confessions of the unsuccessful. I would hear people make excuses for their station in life and I'd make a mental note. I heard the same claims from hundreds, even thousands, as to why life has treated them unfairly. I'm sure you've heard them too. Things like, "I was born on the wrong side of the tracks," "I'm not smart enough," "I could never do that," and the popular, "Some people get all the breaks."

Self-image is one of the first things that must be addressed in order to succeed.

"For as he thinks in his heart, so is he." —Proverbs 23:7(a)

Self-reflection will tell you if there are some things that need to be unlearned that will free you from your perpetual holding pattern. Maybe subconsciously you are repeating behavior to the point that you are unaware that you are hurting your progress and stunting your growth.

Keeping track of your thoughts, and controlling what you think about almost all the time, will be a great place to start. Self-talk can also be liberating or it can dominate you, depending on what you are saying. Thoughts like, "I can never change, learn, lose weight, save money, or start a business" can destroy real progress. And, make no mistake, changing your thought patterns is not an easy task but certainly not impossible either. Thoughts become dynamic once you spend time on them and mix them with emotion whether positive or negative.

About now you must be wondering, how can I change my negative self-sabotaging thoughts and behavior? Simply by replacing them with other thoughts over a period of time. A key to changing your thoughts can be found in Genesis 22:5, *"And Abraham said to his young men, 'Stay here with the donkey; the lad] and I will go yonder and worship, and we will come back to you.'"* How does this scripture apply, you may be asking? If you don't think negatively your life won't be impacted with all those impossible scenarios you've been dwelling on. In other words, you'll stop building a case against yourself. You see, Abraham knew God and His character. He therefore trusted Him enough to declare that after worshipping the Lord, he and the lad would return. He knew the promise God had made to him about Isaac being the seed of many and he didn't doubt it. Worshipping God definitely keeps you focused on the promises of God.

* * * *

WORSHIPPING GOD DEFINITELY KEEPS YOU FOCUSED ON THE PROMISES OF GOD!

* * * *

"But God said to Abraham, 'Do not let it be displeasing in your sight because of the lad or because of your bondwoman. Whatever Sarah has said to you, listen to her voice; for in Isaac your seed shall be called.'" —Genesis 21:12

"No longer shall your name be called Abram, but your name shall be Abraham; for I have made you a father of many nations. I will make you exceedingly fruitful; and I will make nations of you, and kings shall come from you. And I will establish My covenant between Me and you and your descendants after you in their generations, for an everlasting covenant, to be God to you and your descendants after you. Also I give to you and your descendants after you the land in which you are a stranger, all the land of Canaan, as an everlasting possession; and I will be their God."
—Genesis 17:5-8

"Then God said: 'No, Sarah your wife shall bear you a son, and you shall call his name Isaac; I will establish My covenant with him for an everlasting covenant, and with his descendants after him.'" —Genesis 17:19

The biggest breakthroughs in my life came through the changes I made in the way I thought about things. Think about this for a moment. You are in control of your life! You control your decisions and your decisions control your future. Simple yet dynamic, right? You're in control so **STOP** doing what is hurting your future. It could be overeating or not exercising or listening to songs that foster depression. Whatever it is, you are in control of your next move.

YOU ARE IN CONTROL OF YOUR NEXT MOVE!

Attitude and action is everything. Attitude and action helps set the compass of our existence. I once met a man that was an attorney before he flew Jets in the US Airforce and he was a skilled guitar player, practiced Yoga, and was an all around really good person. His attitude is what set him apart from most. He was an excellent, accomplished person, but his attitude was the thing that defined his accomplishments in life.

We only get one shot at life. The thing that not only defines us, but directs our life is our attitude. Socrates said that an unexamined life is not worth living, and he is positively right! Too many people go through life handicapped because they never ask themselves the right question, or any questions for that matter! Questions like: What is the meaning of life? What am I good at? What gifts do I have naturally? What will define happiness for me? Why am I here on earth? These are very important questions to ask ourselves because God never meant for us to just exist, He meant for us to have life, and more abundant according to John 10:10,

> "I came that **they** may have and enjoy **life**, and have it in abundance [**to thefull**, till it overflows]."   —AMP

That is a far cry from the kind of life that many people are living today. And it all starts with having the right attitude. Unsuccessful people have a flaw, it's called a bad attitude. They hate what they do, they dread each day, they lament their choices and are filled with regret. Their productivity in life is mirrored by their outlook in life, both are negative. King Solomon went through many transformations in his life. He started out as a young man hopelessly in love with a woman, and deeply in love with his God. His attitude overflows with devotion, commitment and love. There's no inkling of an attitude that anything other than pure devotion and dedication to God's will for his life. He was young and passionate about God and it is expressed in every word of the book Song of Solomon.

By the time he pens the book of Proverbs he is older and seasoned in the things of God. His wisdom is apparent, and is known throughout the world according to the Queen of Sheba in 1 King 10. She comes all the way from her own country, and in verse 6 she declares:

> *"The report which I heard in my own land about your words and wisdom is true!"*

The book of Proverbs is 31 chapters filled with life lessons, and godly wisdom. What excellent examples Song of Solomon and the book of Proverbs are, showing that Solomon had an excellent relationship with God and man. His attitude, expectation, grace and above all excellence speak in his absence, and is evident to all around him.

But something went very wrong between the book of Proverbs and Ecclesiastes. The book of Ecclesiastes has a completely different tone from the previous 2 books. Now, instead of being passionately in love with his God, and God's ways, Solomon shifts his attitude to everything "under the sun." Solomon looks for love in all the wrong places, as the in the hit song in 1984 by Johnny Lee "Looking For Love." God asked Solomon in 1 Kings 3:5, *"Ask [Me] what I shall give you."*

Solomon could have asked God for anything! Imagine that for a moment! Here in the beginning of Solomon's reign his heart was so pure and sincere, he asked God for wisdom so he could govern God's people successfully. I've heard a lot of prayers from a lot of folks over my 3 decades in ministry, I've never heard one like this!

Solomon's attitude somehow changed from 1 Kings 3:5 because by the book of Ecclesiastes we see a completely different Solomon. In the Song of Solomon the theme is love. In the book of Proverbs it's theme is Wisdom and right living, but not so much in Ecclesiastes. The book of Ecclesiastes starts out in verse 2 stating that *"Vanity of vanities, all is vanity."* Wow, that's quite a transformation in attitude! Now instead of love and wisdom, everything in life has turned to vanity. One of the meanings of the word vanity is "hollow." Now, life had become hollow for Solomon. Somehow Solomon's attitude devolved. He went from, "God, Your will be done," to "My will be done." The old saying that attitude dictates altitude is absolutely correct. Solomon went from displaying such a love for God, to a life that he called hollow. At first he must have caught his love for God from his father King David who would dance before the Lord with sheer abandon, to the point where his wife criticized him for being too expressive. Michal his wife even accused King David of making of fool of himself! (2 Samuel 6:20),

"How glorious was the king of Israel today, uncovering himself today in the eyes of the maids of his servants, as one of the base fellows shamelessly uncovers himself!"

That sounds like a bitter woman to me! That comment didn't affect David though, he truly loved God, and I believe he conveyed it to his children.

Life isn't meaningless or vain. There are just no shortcuts in life. The quickest way to a good attitude is to remember who God is. The quickest path to a terrible attitude is like Solomon, getting involved with 1,000 women, having endless resources to pursue every pleasure in life, wine, women and song. It brought nothing but pain and emptiness to Solomon. A bad attitude can take you places you never wanted to go. Solomon morphed into someone unrecognizable when compared to his younger years when he was filled with love and wisdom. Solomon's attitude went south when his thinking went south. According to Ecclesiastes 1:14 his focus was to turned to everything "under the sun." It went from inspiration to information. He began to look at all the wrong places instead of looking up to God and His kingdom. He changed his view in his old age to things under the sun. We must always be looking up above to the Son instead of the sun. His attitude changed when he stopped looking to God. Today, this moment, we all have the power of choice to see things from above. We have the choice to see things from above, from God's perspective (Psalm 2:4). We get to choose from what perspective we see things. Do we see things from a fallen defeated world view, or from a resurrected, victorious viewpoint. It is for each one of us to decide. A good attitude pays great dividends. A bad attitude costs us a great price.

> *"If you are willing and obedient, You shall eat the good of the land;"* —Isaiah 1:19

We don't get to pick our parents. Maybe you were taught all wrong about how to think, act and react. But, you can choose to take control and find new mentors through relationships, books, seminars and blogs that can bring about a paradigm shift in your life. Stop believing the lie that you are not in control of your future. Also remember that making the right decisions in life will not get you a better life unless you act on those decisions. Those who say they can and those who say they can't are both right!

My wife has said for years that a person's actions can speak so loudly that oftentimes you cannot hear what that person is saying. Knowing what to do is useless separated from action!

●　　●　　●　　●

KNOWING WHAT TO DO IS USELESS SEPARATED FROM ACTION!

●　　●　　●　　●

You are facing another twenty-four-hour day. We've established that it is action that separates the successful from the unsuccessful. Don't do what the unsuccessful do. Don't wait for everything to be convenient before you act. Take time to worship God for where you are and where you're going, for your goals along with what He is doing in your life.

Do not be unwise and thoughtless.

"Therefore do not be foolish and thoughtless, but understand and firmly grasp what the will of the Lord is."

—Ephesians 5:17 (Amp)

* *

THE KEEP IT SIMPLE MENTALITY IS DON'T DO WHAT THE UNSUCCESSFUL DO!

3

SEE WHAT OTHERS DON'T SEE

Helen Keller was born with mountains of obstacles yet she wound up making a real difference in the world. The only thing worse than being born blind is having sight but no vision, said Helen Keller.

· · · ·

THE ONLY THING WORSE THAN BEING BORN BLIND IS HAVING SIGHT BUT NO VISION

· · · ·

"Now it came to pass after these things that God tested Abraham, and said to him, 'Abraham!' And he said, 'Here I am.' Then He said, 'Take now your son, your only son Isaac, whom you love, and go to the land of Moriah, and offer him there as a burnt offering on one of the mountains of which I shall tell you.' So Abraham rose early in the morning and saddled his donkey, and took two of his young men with him, and Isaac his son; and he split the wood for the burnt offering, and arose and went to the place of which God had told him." —Genesis 22:1-3

Obstacles are what you see when you get your eyes off your vision. Verse 4, *"Then on the third day Abraham lifted his eyes and saw the place afar off."*

Looking at the legal paper, I saw the words written in capitals, "See What Others Don't See." Immediately after that sentence was the underlined word, "Opportunities." During one of our sessions together, I asked him to explain what that meant. He told me that people walk right by million dollar ideas every day. He said boldly, "Problems and opportunities come in pairs. You can't have one without the other. If you can figure out how to fix people's problems, you can get paid".

He said, "I began to look at opportunities others either ignored or never considered and I saw that there are diamonds hidden in plain view everywhere.

You just have to train yourself to see them."

He went on to explain. "Like the first job I had as a page boy."

I interrupted to ask what exactly that was.

"A message delivery boy for Western Union," he explained. "Messages had to be delivered by hand all over the island. I got an old bike and made money every day. I also got information daily."

He smiled as he continued, "I learned who needed what and when and how much they were willing to pay someone for it. I was like the Tom Sawyer of my part of town. I'd deliver messages to people and then get side jobs by doing what needed to be done. By the time I was twelve I had a real business going."

His fascinating tale really caught my attention. He went on. "I had bought and sold five cars before I was fourteen. I delivered a Western Union message to a man at the lumberyard. I overheard him voice his need to have scrap wood hauled away each week from his business. I noticed the need I asked him what he would pay and he hired me. I knew a man with a truck so I hired the man with a truck and we both made money. For two decades we have both made a good living from this one lumber yard."

"This same man hauled scrap metal on another job and we both made money from that job too. I leased a small piece of land and sold cars on it by consignment before I even had a driver's license. Before long a local businessman took a liking to me and began to mentor me. In fact, I had amassed enough money by the time I was sixteen to go into partnership with this gentleman for my first real estate on Front Street. I was off and running."

He ended by encouraging me. "Just start seeing what others are missing. There are diamonds everywhere that people will be walking right past. Instead of looking for instant gratification, look for instant ideas!"

INSTEAD OF LOOKING FOR INSTANT GRATIFICATION, LOOK FOR INSTANT IDEAS!

Abraham saw what others missed. There were others with Abraham and they never noticed a thing. That tells me that most everyone sees but many never notice the opportunity. Many see what is and not what can be. I love how the scripture puts it in Genesis 22:4, *"Then on the third day Abraham lifted his eyes and saw the place afar off."*

Abraham looked up. That is exactly what gets and keeps most people down...not looking up. You get a sense of optimism with Abraham. He's on a three-day journey to a destination he's not quite sure about. He is looking up. When was the last time you looked up for help, even when it was difficult? Now that is real faith. It takes someone who understands God and that He always has a plan. It's been said that, "when you're down to nothing, God is up to something."

Abraham's understanding of God's character was all he needed to look up. We just have to train ourselves to see what others are missing! If you don't understand God's character and that He loves you and is for you, it is easy to miss the message in the messes of life.

* * * *

WE JUST HAVE TO TRAIN OURSELVES TO SEE WHAT OTHERS ARE MISSING!

* * * *

"For God so loved the world that He gave His only begotten Son, that whoever believes in Him should not perish but have everlasting life." —John 3:16

One of the worst things we can do is begin to blame God for our station in life. God is good and He has a future and a destiny for you. God has a future and a life filled with hope for all of us, but He also gave us the power and freedom of choice.

"For I know the thoughts that I think toward you, says the Lord, thoughts of peace and not of evil, to give you a future and a hope." —Jeremiah 29:11

"I call heaven and earth as witnesses today against you, that I have set before you life and death, blessing and cursing; therefore choose life, that both you and your descendants may live;" —Deuteronomy 30:19

This is such a powerful scripture because it reveals how God places the responsibility of choice squarely in our hands. Each of us wakes up every day and chooses to worry or trust, overeat or discipline our appetites, give or be stingy, work or play. That's why using the phrase "If it's God's will, He will just do it," is truly shirking your responsibility. Since God has given you and me the power of choice, it is time to ask yourself what you are doing with your power. Plot a course, get a plan and a strategy and then work on it!

Once you have eyes that see and not just look, you will discover opportunities all around you. I knew as a small boy that God had a future and a hope for me so I stayed encouraged.

I thought a lot about the subject of seeing and observing what others overlook. I readied myself to ask him a question that, once answered, would change my life. I asked, " Is there a common trait in successful people's lives that they all have regardless of geography, education, race, economics or background?"

He quickly answered, "Yes". He answered, "they act." Successful people are action minded and goal oriented. Once successful people see an opportunity or know what they should do, they do whatever it takes to keep the vision before their eyes."

He went on to tell me, "In other words, they write down their goals and review them on a regular basis. Once successful people know what they should do and look towards their goals, they are single minded in their pursuit of them."

If you want to know what the weather is, you can open an app on your phone or computer and it tells you what to expect over the next several days. If you want to know what your future holds, check out what you look at, what you think about and what your mind gravitates towards. If you catch yourself worrying and wondering about the future, it should tell you that you are not focused on the goal and the destination you truly desire.

"For as he thinks in his heart, so is he."   —Proverbs 23:7(a)

As I studied the lives of successful people, I read that Andrew Carnegie commissioned a young man, Napoleon Hill, to study the lives of five hundred successful men of his era to find out if there were similarities or habits of these men. Hill came back after his research and reported to Mr. Carnegie that there was indeed a common thread in their lives. They all wrote down their dreams and goals and rehearsed them regularly.

I read of a lady that wanted to be financially successful. She just started going to the local malls and observing the teens that were there, the clothes they were wearing, the gadgets they were using. She saw what was popular and invested in the companies through buying stock. She has become a millionaire by seeing what others were missing in plain sight.

That certainly is one of the keys to succeeding in every area of life. That is how to keep your dreams alive. That is how you keep persevering even in tough times.

> *"Then the Lord answered me and said: 'Write the vision and make it plain on tablets, that he may run who reads it. For the vision is yet for an appointed time; But at the end it will speak, and it will not lie. Though it tarries, wait for it; Because it will surely come, It will not tarry.'"* —Habakkuk 2:2-3

The Bible tells us many times that having a vision is important in order to navigate this life.

> *"Where there is no vision, the people perish:"*
> —Proverbs 29:18(a) (KJV)

The word vision simply means prophetic revelation. Why do some people change careers every two to three years and others stay the course and seem very content? A prophetic revelation can sometimes be the reason. There was something revealed to them.

Time to ask yourself another hard question! What are you supposed to do with the rest of your life? The Bible will give you the general goals that God has for all His children's lives.

- Salvation—1 Timothy 2:4, *"who desires all men to be saved and to come to the knowledge of the truth."*
- Health—Psalm 103:3, *"Who forgives all your iniquities, Who heals all your diseases,"*
- Peace—John 14:27, *"Peace I leave with you, My peace I give to you; not as the world gives do I give to you. Let not your heart be troubled, neither let it be afraid."*
- Prosperity—Deuteronomy 8:18, *"And you shall remember the Lord your God, for it is He who gives you power to get wealth, that He may establish His covenant which He swore to your fathers, as it is this day."*

- Favor—Psalm 84:11(a), *"For the Lord God is a sun and shield; The Lord bestows grace and favor and honor;"*

The Bible clearly tells us the general will of God. To get a specific direction for your life, you must go to the source and ask the hard questions that only God can answer. He answers in many different ways. It can be in a very spectacular way that is so obvious and in your face or it could be as simple as a desire that just won't go away.

When I prayed to God to show me what I should do with my life, He showed me in a very obvious way that even I couldn't miss it. I've written in detail about it in my book, "Keys to Maximizing Your Harvest." The important thing here is to find out what you are supposed to do with your life. Have a vision, a direction and an overriding awareness of purpose from God for your life.

All the greats who have accomplished wonderful things in business, the arts, education and ministry have had a driving force, a call, goals and vision that have dominated their thoughts. If you are ever going to change your world, it will start by changing yourself. Old and bad habits, wasting time, energy and resources are just some of the first changes that must be made. Purpose and passion will change the landscape of your life. Our time on earth is finite so making these changes now ensures that your time to accomplish success does not run out. Make sure you're spending your life on the things that really count. Leo Tolstoy, author of *War and Peace*, said, "Everyone thinks of changing the world, but no one thinks of changing himself."

IF YOU ARE EVER GOING TO CHANGE YOUR WORLD, IT WILL START BY CHANGING YOURSELF!

Choose today to follow an awareness of a God given purpose!

We are either being driven by our goals and dreams or our lack of them. There are people I know personally who are so negative that they might as well, as the saying goes, "stick their heads in the sand like an ostrich." These people see no opportunities and are so negative they cast a shadow of doubt wherever they go.

They have no hope and roam about like doubt magnets.

It is wise to watch your attitude.

"Keep your heart with all diligence, For out of it spring the issues of life." —Proverbs 4:23

The world is a very negative place. It is full of terrorism, hatred, sickness, poverty and greed. If you are not careful and if you don't guard your heart, you will buy into that negative brand of life. You'll only see the bad. Once you've bought into it, you exchange the dream God has for you for the bondage. Negative people and circumstances are contagious so we must be goal and destiny driven. Guard your heart from all the negative and keep feeding your heart and soul with the promises of God.

"A good man out of the good treasure of his heart brings forth good things, and an evil man out of the evil treasure brings forth evil things." —Matthew 12:35

You determine what you are full of! That is why the Bible teaches us to think on the right things.

"Be anxious for nothing, but in everything by prayer and supplication, with thanksgiving, let your requests be made known to God; and the peace of God, which surpasses all understanding, will guard your hearts and minds through Christ Jesus. Finally, brethren, whatever things are true, whatever things are noble, whatever things are just, whatever things are pure, whatever things are lovely, whatever things are of good report, if there is any virtue and if there is anything praiseworthy—meditate on these things."
—Philippians 4:6-8

Life is choice driven and you and I get to determine what the dominating motivation in your life is. It is either purpose, goals and dreams driven or fear anxiety and failure driven. Choose to see what others won't.

> *"to know the love of Christ which passes knowledge; that you may be filled with all the fullness of God. Now to Him who is able to do exceedingly abundantly above all that we ask or think, according to the power that works in us,"*
> —Ephesians 3:19-20

It is very important to be full of God and His desire for your life. Then you will be doing exceedingly and abundantly far above and beyond all you could ask or think. This all begins with what you are thinking and what you are believing for your life.

Here is something that I am convinced of. Until you hear from God, you won't act in a dynamic way. I like what I heard said years ago, "Until you see the light, you won't feel the heat." In the Book of Acts we see that Saul changed direction in a nanosecond once he heard from God. He then got a new direction.

> *"Then Saul, still breathing threats and murder against the disciples of the Lord, went to the high priest"*   —Acts 9:1

> *"As he journeyed he came near Damascus, and suddenly a light shone around him from heaven. Then he fell to the ground, and heard a voice saying to him, 'Saul, Saul, why are you persecuting Me?' And he said, 'Who are You, Lord?' Then the Lord said, 'I am Jesus, whom you are persecuting. It is hard for you to kick against the goads.' So he, trembling and astonished, said, 'Lord, what do You want me to do?' Then the Lord said to him, 'Arise and go into the city, and you will be told what you must do.'"*   —Acts 9:3-6

Saul not only saw the light, he felt the heat. Once we truly get into the presence of God, we will be like Saul also, asking, "Lord, what do you want me to do?" Until it is settled within us, we are really only asking this one life question.

"How do I find out what I'm supposed to do with my life?" As I have stated before, ask God.

"Yet you do not have because you do not ask." —James 4:2(b)

Whenever I am asked the question about a person's destiny or what they should do with their life, I always point them to God. He made you, He knows you, He's got a plan for you; ask God for direction. It could be as subtle as a recurring dream, thought or desire that doesn't go away.

Once you have a direction, write it down and look at it frequently. Think about it continually. Then, finally, find people who have done it successfully and model them.

"Then the Lord answered me and said: 'Write the vision and make it plain on tablets, that he may run who reads it. For the vision is yet for an appointed time; But at the end it will speak, and it will not lie. Though it tarries, wait for it; Because it will surely come, It will not tarry.'" —Habakkuk 2:2-3

Write it, make it plain, run with it, read it, there is an appointed time!

If you're going to see what others don't see, you are going to have to have a process to grow and a process of keeping your dream before your eyes. Personal growth and development will ensure that when the appointed time comes, you are ready for promotion. You can't wait to grow and mature in your life for the appointed time before you begin because you will be crushed either by pride, lust, abuse of power or money. Preparation time is not wasted time, it is part of God's process. In fact, growth is essential to the appointed time. You would never bring a newborn baby home from the hospital, give the baby your American Express card and then leave on vacation to the Caribbean. That is because it is not time for a vacation but time to raise the baby. A process and infrastructure need to be implemented to guarantee proper nutrition and development for the child.

Preparation time is not wasted time.

• • • •

PREPARATION TIME IS NOT WASTED TIME!

• • • •

There are so many great pastors, life coaches and encouragers available to help you find a plan and process for your personal growth. Your future demands you grow. It is time to determine to become the person you have dreamt of being by studying and consistency, while visualizing yourself as that person and looking toward your future. I love what Dr. I. V. Hilliard says, "You can visit your future on the canvas of your imagination." In fact, it is scriptural to imagine or visualize your future. After all, who do you think gave you an imagination?

> "After these things the word of the Lord came to Abram in a vision, saying, 'Do not be afraid, Abram. I am your shield, your exceedingly great reward.' But Abram said, 'Lord God, what will You give me, seeing I go childless, and the heir of my house is Eliezer of Damascus?'"   —Genesis 15:1-2

> "Then He brought him outside and said, 'Look now toward heaven, and count the stars if you are able to number them.' And He said to him, 'So shall your descendants be.' And he believed the Lord, and He accounted it to him for righteousness."   —Genesis 15:5-6

> "blessing I will bless you, and multiplying I will multiply your descendants as the stars of the heaven and as the sand which is on the seashore; and your descendants shall possess the gates of their enemies. In your seed all the nations of the earth shall be blessed, because you have obeyed My voice."   —Genesis 22:17-18

God gave Abraham the stars in the sky, the sands of the desert and the seashore as illustrations so he could imagine his offspring to come on the earth.

It is what you do every day that really counts.

* * * *

IT IS WHAT YOU DO EVERY DAY THAT COUNTS!

* * * *

"For as he thinks in his heart, so is he [in behavior—one who manipulates]." —Proverbs 23:7(a) (Amp)

Growth is a must! Without it you plateau, stop growing and slowly slip into old habits of existing instead of dominating. It is time to understand that God's original plan was for all His children to dominate their lives, not be dominated. We must see what others miss.

"Then God said, 'Let Us make man in Our image, according to Our likeness; let them have dominion over the fish of the sea, over the birds of the air, and over the cattle, over all the earth and over every creeping thing that creeps on the earth.' So God created man in His own image; in the image of God He created him; male and female He created them. Then God blessed them, and God said to them, 'Be fruitful and multiply; fill the earth and subdue it; have dominion over the fish of the sea, over the birds of the air, and over every living thing that moves on the earth.' And God said, 'See, I have given you every herb that yields seed which is on the face of all the earth, and every tree whose fruit yields seed; to you it shall be for food.'" —Genesis 1:26-29

For many, they have to see it for themselves before they will believe. The Bible clearly teaches that we can lose ground in our lives by being disengaged.

"But he who looks into the perfect law of liberty and continues in it, and is not a forgetful hearer but a doer of the work, this one will be blessed in what he does."   —James 1:25

"that you do not become sluggish, but imitate those who through faith and patience inherit the promises."

—Hebrews 6:12

I have spent a great deal of money on books, teachings and seminars to help me grow and develop. In fact, every successful person usually does. It is a daily thing. Your future will be filled with bigger and bigger mountains and giants and it is important to grow beyond your obstacles. My dad used to say, "The way to eat an elephant is one bite at a time." That is exactly how you grow, one day at a time!

Have a vision and a dream, commit to growing personally, spiritually and intellectually. Stay with it, be persistent. Become observant and see your destiny that is hidden in your habits.

In Habakkuk we saw that we need to write the vision (goal or dream) and make it plain. Then we need to run with it which means there must be action. Continually read what you've written as you go forward toward your appointed time. Keep reading it, keep rehearsing it and see it. And, just as Abraham looked at the stars each night and reminded himself that he was going to be the father of a great multitude without having even one child, do the same.

Your vision or goal will take you to a place worth going. All my books started as dreams in my heart first. Buildings are first seen in someone's heart, then on a blueprint before they are ever built.

I remember attending a meeting where Tommy Barnett said, "The greatest churches in America haven't been built yet." He then asked us if we would be the one who builds one of them. The man standing next to me said, "I'll be one of them!" And he was. He could see it. He had a large church in his heart as a dream and a goal. He saw it before it came to pass.

What are your goals? Are they a debt free home and car? How about a large savings account or a healthy body that is in shape and free of excess weight? Maybe they are a happy home and several businesses? Whatever your dreams, write the vision and make it plain! This way you can look at it and ultimately run with it.

WRITE THE VISION AND MAKE IT PLAIN!

The only thing holding you back from a better future is information, motivation and a process. Zig Ziglar once said, "We have to get rid of stinking thinking and we need a checkup from the neck up." Keep in mind that those who say they can and those who say they can't are both right!

Having a dream, looking at it and visualizing it coming to pass, coupled with growth as a person are all part of the process. This also requires us to eliminate the stinking thinking from our past. You see, thinking can hold you back as well as free you for a prosperous future. It all depends on your perspective.

My new friend drove me over and parked in the lot of a building and told me about his first office building he was thinking of buying. It seemed like a mountain that was too high to climb. He thought it was a risk that was too large. He said his mentor met him on the property and walked it with him, helping him see the value of the opportunity and the potential of the prime location and square footage of the space. It took someone with experience to help him see the value. And after a thirty-minute meeting he realized he'd be hurting himself and missing out on an incredible opportunity if he passed on it. You've got to see it!

As an example, we've all been to the circus and have seen the big elephant tied up with a little rope around his ankle that is secured by a peg hammered into the ground. You and I both know that a large elephant that can weigh upwards of seven tons could easily pull up that rope and rip the peg out of the ground. I've read that as babies, these elephants have sharp chains tied around their ankles that cut into their skin when they pulled against the chains. After a while, their skin would be cut deep and raw and, through this pain, they learned not to put any tension on the chains. They became conditioned to associate pain with putting pressure on their ankles which were tied to the pegs or posts in the ground. Because of this conditioning, there is no longer a need for heavy chains and that is why a mere rope is sufficient to keep them tied down.

Many need to realize that we've all been conditioned by the world, the devil, negative experiences, family and friends not to push for success or look to fulfill our dreams. The premise is either to avoid the pain of discipline or a past failure or what might happen in the future. Pretty soon we find that we have settled for less and have stopped dreaming and setting goals for ourselves. We've failed to understand that the entire time, just like the seven ton elephant, we had the ability to pull up the status quo and simply go for gold. We've had what it takes all along to run the race and receive the prize. We merely have to press beyond our comfort zone and see what others don't see.

WE'VE HAD WHAT IT TAKES ALL ALONG TO RUN THE RACE AND RECEIVE THE PRIZE

Charles Holland Duell was the commissioner of the U.S. Patent and Trademark office from 1898 to 1901. Later he served as a federal judge. Duell was the one credited for saying, "Everything that can be invented has been invented." Sounds a bit of a stretch that a man of his intellect, that ran a patent office would say such a thing! Even in his day Duell's office had thousands of applications for a patent annually. Today hundreds of thousands of new patents are submitted annually. Somehow that statement "Everything that can be invented has been invented" made it's way into a 1987 speech by

Ronald Reagan[1]. Duell probably never really made that statement[2], but it was attributed to him. It was a quote that was actually taken from a comedy magazine. In 1902 Duell did say, "In my opinion, all previous advancements in the various lines of invention will appear totally insignificant when compared with those which the present century will witness. I almost wish that I might live my life over again to see the wonders which are at the threshold." He was anticipating many new inventions and breakthroughs that would benefit mankind.

My wife and I live in Fort Myers, Florida. The winter home of Thomas Edison is here. He was a master at seeing what others didn't see. It is said he tried for many years to create the incandescent light bulb. We toured his laboratory in Fort Myers. He was so committed to his project he ate and slept in the lab many times. He attempted to create the light bulb several thousand times. Finally he saw what he had been missing. He never looked at his previous attempts as failures. He was quoted as saying "I just found many ways you couldn't invent the light bulb." He saw things differently than others. He has 2,332 patents world wide.

What are you waiting for to begin to see things differently than you have for all these years? There's no time like the present to start choosing to see "the cup" not only half full, but overflowing. Successful people choose to develop their mind and cultivate their thinking. Albert Einstein was 26 years old when he wrote The Theory of Relativity. Martin Luther King, Jr. was 34 years old when he wrote his famous speech "I Have A Dream." Mozart was competent on keyboard and violin by age 5. The Wright Brothers, Orville (32) and Wilbur (36) invented and built the first successful airplane and flew it. It's not up to God for you to see what others don't see, It's up to you! He gives us the power of choice each day to lift our gaze above the horizon and dream of what could be.

---

1   www.presidency.ucsb.edu/ws/?pid=35547

2   https://www.quora.com/

Nothing is more powerful than a thought that becomes more than just a thought. Nothing moves man more than a possibility than can become reality. It is more than being optimistic, it's more than motivation. It's faith that God has a better, brighter day for you. Being able to see with an eye of faith carries you through storms. Seeing beyond what is, raises you to a level of someone who is unstoppable. Moses was able to see beyond the Red Sea, and Manna. Rahab the harlot could see that God was at work in the lives of the Israelites and chose the people of God rather than the people of Jericho. David saw beyond the 5 smooth stones in his bag, he saw himself defeat the giant Goliath. You can too see beyond where you're at today. We are supernatural beings blessed by God to be able to see beyond what is to what can be. It's a choice to have the spiritual backbone to look up when you feel down.

There are diamonds all over the ground that most people aren't noticing. Your dream and your future is out there waiting for you. Write the vision, make it plain, run after it and keep reading your goals. Be patient and wait for the appointed time.

THE KEEP IT SIMPLE MENTALITY IS SEE WHAT OTHERS DON'T SEE!

4

FOCUS

About half way down the legal page was a single word that was underlined and highlighted with an orange marker. It boldly stated FOCUS. I spent the day with my new mentor and as we were driving around running errands, I asked him about the single word Focus on the sheet of paper he'd given me. He pulled his Bentley over in the parking lot of another building he owned and gave me a fifteen-minute seminar right there on what it is to be truly focused. If anyone wants to succeed they must control three areas of their lives. Success and failure are not a game of chance but choice. He said learn to: 1. Control your thoughts; 2. Learn to control your words; and finally, 3. Learn to control your feelings. All three must be focused in order to succeed.

He began by saying, "Focus or the lack thereof can be the greatest asset, or the greatest enemy to your future. Having too many options can be a detriment to any success because they are distractions." His words brought back a story I had heard many years ago about Sadhu Sundar Singh, an Indian Minister in the early 1900's. He was invited to America by one of our religious denominations. He came to America by ship, which in those days took over one month. They had made advanced arrangements for a full year of meetings at different churches and revivals around the country. When he disembarked the ship, he had one hour to wait for his contact to arrive to meet him so he decided to walk around the streets of New York City. He was stunned at all the busyness and preoccupation with materialism he saw along with the total dysfunction of the people in the city. He listened to the conversations and the squabbles and the confusion of the city. Sadhu grabbed his bag and went right back to board the ship to return home. He stated: "The US is too busy and distracted for a real move of God."

A lack of focus can cripple your dreams and sabotage your future and effectiveness. It doesn't matter whether you are a Fortune 500 CEO, or a major league batter, a hair stylist or a race car driver; never lose your focus!

Bill Gates was once asked what he considered to be the number one skill for success. He answered without hesitation that it was focus. A key take away from this chapter is to appreciate the value of each moment, to focus on the task at hand and learn what is important. Eckhart Tolle once said[3], "All negativity is caused by an accumulation of psychological time and denial of the present. Unease, anxiety, tension, stress, worry—all forms of fear—are caused by too much future, and not enough presence. Guilt, regret, resentment, grievances, sadness, bitterness, and all forms of non-forgiveness are caused by too much past, and not enough presence. Spend time honing the important skill of focus. The majority of people you meet in life have a habit of living in the past. They focus on what's behind them and not what's out in front of them. They're afraid of making mistakes therefore they stop taking chances. Instead of focusing on their dreams and their future they rely on their past faulty experience trying to avoid any discomfort, or have a fear of the unknown. There's struggle in any future worth pursuing. The day you stop focusing on your dreams is the day you start growing old. When you're focused you establish a 'No Excuse Zone.'"

---

3   Eckhart Tolle, *The Power of Now: A Guide to Spiritual Enlightenment*

SPEND TIME HONING THE
IMPORTANT SKILLS OF FOCUS!

Become a master in these three areas of life and you'll change any circumstances you're faced with. Ignore them and you'll be at the mercy of circumstances and dominated by the pressures of the day.

1. CONTROL YOUR THOUGHTS OR BE CONTROLLED BY THEM

Your thinking should be pro-active. The majority of people you come in contact with in life respond to what they think off the top of their heads, without truly examining what they're thinking about. Proverbs 23:7 states: *"As He thinks in His Heart so is He."* So the biblical principal is: As you think, so you become! Romans 8:6 states: *"For to be carnally minded is death but to be spiritually minded is life and peace."* The spiritual law here is you can choose your thoughts. And if you choose the right thoughts you'll have real life and peace. You can and should choose your thoughts because they become your reality. I may get a lot of pushback for this statement, but I believe fears, depression, anxiety and phobias are all learned behaviors. There are only two fears any of us are born with: 1. Fear of loud noises; 2. The fear of falling. All the other fears are learned. And they all started with a thought. Inside that three pound brain of ours is the mind, emotions, the will, the intellect and the imagination. There is also the conscience, which I believe to be the voice of the renewed human spirit once it is made alive at salvation. All these can and must be developed to guarantee maximized performance. Most people don't spend any time or resources developing their minds and fall pray to negativity or depression. Prescription drugs used to stabilize people's behavior or moods are at an all time high. The average person falls prey to an idle non-productive mind, but you are not average. I go into much more detail in my book "Keys

To Maximizing Your Harvest" on the subject. If you are ever going to be a high level achiever, you must develop the ability to focus your thoughts. Command your thoughts as a general would his army in battle. You can do it and you must, to separate yourself from the average. Dr. I.V. Hilliard said, "Average gets no attention." The great achievers in history all have focus, and the future won't discriminate against anyone that chooses to learn to focus.

2. THE POWER OF YOUR WORDS.

Proverbs 18:21, *"Death and Life are in the power of the Tongue!"* If you don't believe words control your life stand in front of a judge sometime and hear the word guilty. Stand before a minister and say "I do" or stand before a doctor and hear the word terminal. This is a spiritual and natural law that must be respected and cooperated with. Numerous studies have been done on words and how they affect our every day life. Our bodies and our health are all affected by our words and our beliefs. The Bible teaches that we have the spiritual ability to speak God's word into any situation and change it. David spoke to Goliath and defeated him. (1 Sam. 17:32-37) Jesus spoke to the wind and the waves and they obeyed Him. (Mt.8:23-27) We could go on and on. Mark.11:22-24 teaches to speak to the mountains or problems in life and they will move. You and I have the power of choice to be like our God when you use words, or to be like the devil and speak lies, doubt or fear. Pretty bold statement. You use your words like your creator and speak life to things, circumstances and problems. Or you go with the tide of the moment, good or bad, positive or negative. Acting like God in the middle of the world that hates God is no easy task until you choose to focus. Here are some scriptures for you to read and believe if you're bold enough; words from God's Word that show the power of words. Mark 11:11-14, Mark 11:20-24, Ephesians 5:6, John 6:63, Matthew 12:37, Revelation 12:11, Ro.10:9-10, Job 3:25-26, Job 6:24-25 just to mention a few.

3. FEELINGS

1 Thess.5:22, *"And the very God of peace sanctify you wholly; and I pray your whole spirit and soul and body be preserved blameless unto the coming of our Lord Jesus Christ"*. The sooner we all learn the dynamics and differences of the Spirit, Soul and Body truth, the sooner we can maximize it. You are a spirit. The real you is a spirit that will live on eternally. Now we get to choose where that spirit will live eternally by choosing or rejecting Jesus. So the real you is a spirit. We have a body to contact this natural world. But once we die we are still alive because our spirit is eternal. The spirit and the body are pretty easy to understand but it's the soul that confuses most people. We get our feelings confused with what is our reality. Feelings can and will change from moment to moment. Feeling is the indicator given us by God so that we can constantly monitor our soul. God hard wired us with feelings to alert us to what our dominant thoughts are. If you are feeling blue just check out what you've been thinking about. If you're happy it's because of what you've been meditating on. Most of the emotional problems folks have, is because their thinking is negative and an emotion rises in them. We can reverse that cycle at any moment by choosing a better thought. Try it; you'll like it. (Ep.4:23) *"Be renewed in the spirit of your mind."* (Phil.4:8) *"Whatever things are true, whatever things noble, whatever things are just, whatever things are pure, whatever things are lovely, whatever things are of a good report, if there is any virtue and if there is anything praiseworthy think on these things."* Invest the effort to think about the good things in life and reject the negative of your past. You'll see your emotional life will be full of peace and joy.

It is truly amazing what can be accomplished through focus. A shaft of light that is focused and concentrated becomes a laser beam. Based on this analogy, the amount of focus you apply to your life will produce the goals you've dreamt about.

THE AMOUNT OF FOCUS YOU APPLY TO YOUR LIFE WILL PRODUCE THE GOALS YOU'VE DREAMT ABOUT!

An example of losing focus can be evidenced in the lions' cage at the circus. A question was asked of a lion tamer. "I see you have a whip, a chair and a pistol with you when you are in the cage with the lions and tigers. If you could only have one of them, which would you choose?"

The lion tamer replied, "That's easy, I'd choose the chair. The whip can't stop a lion or a tiger. The gun only has caps in it and could never stop a lion or a tiger either. But, the chair has four legs and the lion tamer always holds the seat end and points the legs at the big cats. When the chair is tilted just a little, it makes the four legs of the chair protrude at different angles. The lions and tigers get distracted because they always focus on the closest thing to them and since all four legs are so close to the same distance from the animal, they get distracted trying to focus on four things at the same time. It is at that point they become as docile as house cats."

It has been said that to stop a person with a dream, merely give them multiple dreams. You see, pursuing many dreams is distracting. Distractions and obstacles are what we see when we have di-vision, we naturally stop chasing our dreams efficiently when we get overloaded. We get maintenance driven instead of purpose and mission driven. Obstacles come to make you lose focus.

We need a plan, a process and focus to succeed!

Protect your focus at all costs. It is the little foxes that ruin the vine, Song of Solomon 2:15, *"Catch us the foxes, the little foxes that spoil the vines, for our vines have tender grapes."* In fact, it is the immediate that crowds out the important.

IT IS THE IMMEDIATE THAT
CROWDS OUT THE IMPORTANT!

Rick Pitino, the legendary college basketball coach tells a story about making a home visit to one of the top recruits in the nation. The coach himself made the visit to help persuade the young man and his family that attending his university and playing for his basketball program was a great choice for him. He did so by sharing the virtues and advantages the young man would have. Imagine with me the advantages and life lessons this young man was being offered as well as a first class college education. Envision the contacts and opportunities that could come this young man's way just by his association with this influential coach.

During the recruiting visit, coach Pitino was extolling the virtues of the university and the basketball program when the young man received a text message on his phone. He answered the text message immediately which told the coach that as good as a player this young man was and with all his talent; he wasn't focused on what was really important at that moment. A huge opportunity was missed by this young man because of a lack of focus. What doors may never open to him again? What contacts and opportunities evaporated when the coach walked out the door? Focus or a lack of it is a game changer.

My eighty-eight-year-old father believed before his death, the biggest regret he had in his lifetime was not understanding the magnitude of a moment. When he was just a young man during WW2 and a new volunteer in the Navy, his job was to serve a high ranking Naval officer. The officer detected that my dad an ensign, had the intellect and the scholastic ability beyond his position in the Navy. The high ranking officer arranged an Appointment at Large for my dad at the Naval Academy at Annapolis. Unfortunately, my dad did not realize the opportunity that was before him and he didn't understand the significance of the high ranking officer's influence and ability to open doors.

He lost focus and passed up the Appointment at Large to the Naval Academy. Seventy years is a long time to lament over missed opportunities. Focus or lack thereof is one of the keys that will make or break your dream.

The best way to stay focused is by having goals and reading them daily! How do we lose focus you may ask? By letting other less important things steal time, attention, energy, resources and creativity away from the goal.

GOAL SETTING

Do you know why the top ten per cent of the wealthiest people in the world are where they are? Because they have goals and they follow them. They look at them, dream about them and rehearse them continually. A goal must be readable if it is going to be reachable! Coach Lou Holtz is one of the best examples of setting goals and achieving them. He may even be the king of goal setting. He set 107 goals over forty years ago and has achieved 105 of them.

A GOAL MUST BE READABLE IF IT IS GOING TO BE REACHABLE!

In the Old Testament, the prophet Habakkuk wrote down his strategic plan to achieve His God given destiny Habakkuk 2:2, *"Then the Lord answered me and said: 'Write the vision and make it plain on tablets, that he may run who reads it.'"* The prevailing theme is to write it down, keep it simple, run with it or have an action plan and keep reading goals over and over! There is something about visiting your goals regularly that keeps you engaged in the process of pursuit. Anyone can write down goals but not everyone will read them daily.

Our futures are hidden inside our routines. Having a piece of double chocolate cake once in a blue moon won't pack on pounds but if you eat the cake every day, it won't be long before your route changes your wardrobe. It is what we do each and every day that counts.

IT IS WHAT WE DO EACH AND EVERY DAY THAT COUNTS!

Everyone you meet has a goal. We all intuitively know that we have a contribution to make while here on earth. We meet people who are worn out, negative, depressed and have given up, yet deep inside them, they know they have something to do beyond the status quo they are living. Our futures are hidden inside our routines.

There are folks who may have no idea how to reach their dreams or obtain the finances they want to have, but if you talk to them long enough, a glimmer of hope, even from the most negative person, will shine through. These statements are not made through the eyes of judgment, but rather in spite of the dog eat dog world we live in. Understanding that life can easily run a swath through us, everyone instinctively knows they are unique and, given the opportunity, even realizes all things are possible and the extraordinary is not beyond your reach.

The prospect of your dreams and goals is the very thing that puts the spring in your step. Think back to your early childhood. Little girls usually dreamt of becoming Miss America or the captain of the cheerleading team and the boys wanted to be astronauts, walk on the moon or hit that game winning home run. None of us dreamt small when we were young. I want to encourage you to dream again. Dream like there is not a chance you won't reach your goal. Take a chance, become vulnerable and dream again.

It may be time to dust off your old journals and start to imagine again. Maybe you lost your focus. It happens because life happens and we have to be like the salmon and swim upstream and against the current. The best way I know how to do this is to remember your goals, rehearse your goals and write down your goals. Many goals fall by the wayside and have been a victim of the stress of life. I want to remind you that there is still life in your goal. Refocus and remember what once excited you!

THERE IS STILL LIFE IN THAT GOAL!

At the beginning and end of each year, I give a series of talks entitled, "How to Finish Strong" and "How to Stay Strong." The first key to finishing anything well is to remember why you started to begin with. Focus is nothing more than giving your attention to something and keeping it there. You can go back and breathe life into your dream again simply by refocusing. Nobody dreamt about struggle or frustration when they were a child. We had to learn frustration and negativity.

Controlling your thoughts, words and feelings are a great way to jump start your focus. Goal setting is one of the greatest vehicles to keep you on track to accomplishing them. Think of this for a moment: Your idea that been down deep in your heart maybe the key to fixing the problem of world hunger or the next great breakthrough in aviation. Your idea could change the world, or it could change someone else's world. My Pastor just passed away a week ago. His life influenced my life and my wife's life in so many ways. His commitment to follow the dreams in his heart changed and challenged our lives. That may sound insignificant to some, but there are thousands of others' lives that have been eternally changed by his choices to follow his dreams and focus.

There's only one reason a dream has been in your soul all these years. It's there to be pursued because the Almighty is thinking of others. If we take a moment to be honest with ourselves, we will agree that we only get one life. That life is disappearing one day at a time. Without focus we will lose decades with busyness and frivolous attempts at being content. Being focused and pursuing your dreams may sound risky but it is much sounder than putting your life in neutral and just enduring another decade. Knuckling under and surviving the life is no life at all. When you're following the dream in your heart you're fulfilling the call of the Lord when He said, "Follow me.." God called frustrated fishermen that had caught nothing after fishing all night long. He called shepherd boys (David) to lead a nation. He called a virgin girl (Mary) to bring a Savior into the world. And He has a plan for you also. It says in Jeremiah 29:11 *"For I know the thoughts that I think toward you, says the Lord, thoughts of peace and not of evil, to give you a future and a hope."*

Don't allow yourself to be overly concerned about your qualifications or lack of them, just stay focused. The early church looked anything other than qualified at it's inception. Led by a rag-tag bunch yet after the day of Pentecost, this group evangelized 51% of the civilized world within a century. What am I getting at here? With focus you and God make the majority. Focus qualifies your dream. God adds everything that you're missing. He knows how to finish what He starts. He's just looking for those that will focus and follow His plan.

God doesn't have a printing press so money isn't going to come floating down from the heavens. God gives you an idea, then you focus and chase your dreams. God adds more information and inspiration. It takes pursuit. God instructed Timothy to study in 2 Timothy 2:15). There must be action before there's any advancement. The focus you give determines much of the progress you make. It's work to improve yourself! My wife and I spend several thousand dollars a year on books, seminars, etc. to improve and focus our lives. Education and ignorance have one thing in common: They're both expensive! You may ask how is ignorance expensive? You'll never know the opportunities you missed because you weren't ready for them and you went unnoticed. Zig Ziglar says it's better to have no opportunity, that to get an opportunity and not be ready. I.V Hilliard says "Average gets no attention." Here's the challenge: will you focus on the important? Or will you major on the minor things in life? Will you simply live by your emotions and allow them to drag you to and fro? Again the choice is yours to make.

Let's get a little strategic amnesia when it comes to the negatives and focus on a preferred future. It is time to remember why you started. Do yourself a favor today. Take some alone time and either re-engage with your old goal or get a new one. Remember why you started in the first place and rehearse it! There is something about repetition that is dynamic.

When I first began to take flying lessons, the instructor made us students do "touch and goes" over and over and over again. We would start the process of landing and would touch the wheels on the runway and then reverse everything. We would then pick up the speed we had lost and take off again. Repetition or rehearsal built muscle memory into our consciousness. After we did this many many times, we all got proficient at taking off and landing. To become an expert, it will take years of rehearsal; but almost everyone could land and take off in a small plane after these run-throughs.

Jack Nicklaus said, "I never hit a shot, not even in practice, without having a very sharp and focused picture of it in my head." Picture yourself fulfilling your goals and dreams. There is something spiritual and dynamic in visualization. Picture your future in your mind to get a snap shot or short vignette. Then replay it in your mind over and over again. It is both powerful and scriptural.

God told Abraham he was going to be the father of a great multitude.

"When Abram was ninety-nine years old, the Lord appeared to Abram and said to him, 'I am Almighty God; walk before

Me and be blameless. And I will make My covenant between Me and you, and will multiply you exceedingly.' Then Abram fell on his face, and God talked with him, saying: 'As for Me, behold, My covenant is with you, and you shall be a father of many nations.''' —Genesis 17:1-4

Yet Abram and his wife Sara had no children and they had biologically run out of time. Still God changed their names and gave them a plan to reignite the dream of a great nation.

"No longer shall your name be called Abram, but your name shall be Abraham; for I have made you a father of many nations. I will make you exceedingly fruitful; and I will make nations of you, and kings shall come from you. And I will establish My covenant between Me and you and your descendants after you in their generations, for an everlasting covenant, to be God to you and your descendants after you. Also I give to you and your descendants after you the land in which you are a stranger, all the land of Canaan, as an everlasting possession; and I will be their God." —Genesis 17:5-8

"Then God said to Abraham, 'As for Sarai your wife, you shall not call her name Sarai, but Sarah shall be her name. And I will bless her and also give you a son by her; then I will bless her, and she shall be a mother of nations; kings of peoples shall be from her.''' —Genesis 17:15-16

He gave them illustrations, pictures and props for them to visualize in their minds. It is not weird, it is biblical. I could give you dozens of examples right out of Scripture to show that rehearsing your dreams and goals helps keep you focused.

Write it. Habakkuk 2:2, *"Write the vision and make it plain..."* I know a man who is always talking about what he is going to do or what he should have done. One day I asked him, "Why don't you stop talking about it and do it?"

I then asked, "Have you ever written down exactly what you want to achieve in goal form?" to which he replied, "No, I haven't because I don't have the time to write it down and read it each day."

The last time I spoke with him, he was talking about yet another plan he had.

You cannot achieve it if you can't read it and see it. Before any skyscraper is built, it is a blueprint on a page. Before any business is built, there is a business plan.

Whenever anyone goes to the bank to borrow money for a new business, the bank wants to see your plan. Let me see your strategic steps and plans to ensure the success of the business venture so I can see the profit potential for my investment. That is simply because it will explain everything I need to know about the plan which will reveal just how serious you are. Those who are truly serious will write down the plan. Goals and dreams are fragile. If they are not given the proper amount of attention, they will shrivel up and die just like small plants in a greenhouse with no water.

REMEMBER YOUR DREAMS, REHEARSE YOUR GOALS AND WRITE THEM DOWN!

I wanted to lose weight for years but I never wrote down a plan. Finally, I got sick and tired of being sick and tired of those extra twenty-five to thirty pounds of excess weight. My wife brought me to reality when she simply asked, "Why not practice what you preach? Set a goal and write it down."

A light bulb went on in my head and I no longer allowed the start to stop me. I made short term, mid-range and long term goals and wrote my goals down. I wrote 'Lose Thirty Pounds' at the top of the page. The first thing I wrote down was to eat right, exercise and do it daily. The results were predictable. I have to admit that nothing happened until I wrote it down and looked at it.

If your goal is not readable, it is not reachable!

I sometimes interchange goals and dreams but there is a definite difference between the two. Dreams are wonderful and are the wishes we have until we attach a strategy and action to them. I have several but I can't choose them all. Writing down your goals helps clarify and focus the dreams. It is writing them both down and rehearsing them that infuses them with life.

WRITING DOWN YOUR GOALS HELP CLARIFY AND FOCUS THE DREAMS!

Dreams are where we want to go. Goals get us there! Focused goals should be challenging as well as attainable. Both Joselyn and myself have learned from Terri Savelle Foy to not only write down our goals but to take it a step further and attach a picture or props to help us see them come to pass. Your dream is your future. Protect it with daily attention even when you don't feel like it. An ounce of action is better than a ton of intention. Feelings are fickle so act even when you are discouraged. That's just part of being an adult. Doing what we don't want to do.

THE KEEP IT SIMPLE MENTALITY IS
DON'T TRUST YOUR FEELINGS!
ACT!

5

FIND A MENTOR—BE A MENTOR

"that you do not become sluggish, but imitate those who through faith and patience inherit the promises."

—Hebrews 6:12

Although that may sound to some to be very general and benign, these words were written in bold red letters and underlined three times on my new mentor's page. I read that statement about the fourth night of my trip and I asked this highly successful man who was my host and had become my friend specifically what he meant by it.

He smiled and said, "If you lie down with the dogs, you will wake up with the fleas."

As we left his office and were driving along he seemed very excited, so I asked him why he was in such a great mood. His answer was refreshing.

He said, "I'm happy because I spent time with people I love this morning and I am optimistic about today. You know, I never get to do this day over again Dan, so I'd better take advantage of it."

He went on to say, "One of my mentors taught me you don't see life as it is, you see it how you are. It was through my mentor's modeling of this optimistic attitude that I learned every day and every person is important."

He explained that because he had pretty much raised himself, he picked up some bad habits, things like not treating people in ways you want to be treated, even when they weren't nice. Or helping people who could never help you. And making a difference where you can because helping others is one of the quickest ways to help yourself.

This humble yet powerful man went on to explain that everyone needs a mentor in life and everyone needs to be a mentor. The most profound thing I learned that day during our car ride was the people first principle. He modeled this people principle as he put it, everywhere he went. As impactful as it was, I understand it much clearer today. He spoke about the many times people went out of their way to help him or to be kind. What he was saying was that there are always people watching us who have the ability to help us. The key is, since you never know who is watching, be good to everyone.

YOU NEVER KNOW WHO IS WATCHING, BE GOOD TO EVERYONE!

He talked about several of his own mentors over the years and during different stages of his career. One mentor helped him with the value of listening and not talking all the time. That was a hard lesson to learn for me since I had developed the knack of over talking because of dyslexia. I've learned that we all have insecurities and because of that we set up emotional infrastructures to protect ourselves as well as diversions so others won't know about our pesky dysfunctions. In fact, I had a real gift and could talk you to death. But, no one ever learns anything when they keep talking. It is only when we listen and act on what we hear that causes growth.

He also talked about another mentor in his life who taught him that an ounce of action is worth more than a ton of talk. After saying this once, he paused and repeated it. He went on to share, "All the talk in the world won't change your life unless you put it to work." Then he quoted Benjamin Franklin, "A man of words and not of deeds is like a garden full of weeds." After all is said and done, there's always more said than done, one person quipped. Only hungry minds grow and growing minds share with others. He said there is nothing more regrettable than unused potential, seeing people waste their lives by choosing not to be mentored.

AN OUNCE OF ACTION IS WORTH MORE THAN A TON OF TALK!

My new friend told me that unless you grow beyond your present circumstances, both emotionally and intellectually, your thinking will stop your next opportunity.

That is why it is a must to set up a plan and a process to grow. I thought about it there in the car as we drove along. If I was really honest with myself, my personal growth plan was kind of hit and miss. When I was inspired I'd read and journal. When I was motivated or condemned, I'd study. But, to say I had a systematic plan for personal growth, no way. If I was ever going to be a mentor to others, I had better find a mentor and get serious about growing emotionally and intellectually.

WHO YOU CHOOSE TO MENTOR YOU IS AS IMPORTANT AS WHO YOU STAY AWAY FROM!

Who you choose to mentor you is as important as who you stay far away from. We can all look back over our lives and see where so-called mentors have held us back or mistreated us.

There are sign posts for people who are truly serious about change. You know someone is serious about personal growth and development when they hire a personal trainer. I've known folks who were one hundred pounds plus overweight and hired a personal trainer. Within a matter of months of instruction, they got themselves in shape and are a picture of health. Why did they make such rapid progress? Because they had someone who had been there and done that and was willing to teach and help them through the myriad of mine fields of weight loss.

You see, mentors know things you and I might not know. They know the signs of stagnation and desperation. They can spot the areas of our lives that we are blinded to. Once I set some priorities like prayer, study of the Word, listening to quality music and teaching, I then set goals and reviewed them regularly. Goals like eating right, exercising and practicing what I preached; I must admit life became better very quickly. Mentors helped me with discipline and goal setting that would have been unachievable in my previous emotional, intellectual and spiritual condition.

Mentors helped me see the value in these areas as well as showed me how I had been sabotaging any progress by waiting for inspiration to act. Having a growth plan changed my life and has helped prepare me for my future. If you're not ready when you get there, you could go unnoticed, or worse, be ignored by the very people who could promote you in life. A growth plan helps you prevent the start and stop, start and stop, start and stop syndrome which the majority of people are in.

Being a mentor and having a mentor are definitely work, but it is worth it! You don't want to become one of those people who sits around year after year talking about their glory days of high school football or cheerleading, what could have been, should have been and what might have been. In fact, your best days can be now and you can help others realize their best days now by mentoring others. Any growing person can mentor someone else.

You can learn every secret to success from every guru there is out there in the self help field. All the secrets will work or none of them will work, depending on if you work them. None of the secrets to success work unless you do. Mentors and mentoring help keep your eyes on the prize.

There is something about serving and helping others that is beyond therapeutic, it's revolutionary and dynamic. My friend was excited about his day because he knew the value and potential of the day. It can bring both opportunity and obstacles and usually does, but his priorities were right. He spent time with the people he loved and his expectant attitude overflowed toward what the day could bring. I've tried to approach each day since then the exact same way and have learned to value relationships and value each day.

Just a few months ago, I was speaking at a national convention. I was in the Green Room talking with some of the other presenters. There were only a few of us left in the room and one of them was an extremely wealthy and successful man who is one of my mentors. In a flash I saw in my mind's eye me presenting a business idea to him. To tell the truth, and looking back on the moment, it was like walking into the Shark Tank TV show. I asked this gentleman to step into an adjoining office and I told him my idea. He loved it and encouraged me to chase my dream. He's helped more than 1000 people with their ideas and dreams and some have become millionaires. Helping people is a staple of his life. Think of that. This one man has helped well over a thousand families live their dream.

And that number has continued to climb ever since.

He has helped me immensely and connected me with movers and shakers in related fields. I needed his mentoring in the project and his tenacity. He's not afraid of anything because he has already entered into projects much larger than this one I had. I need a mentor's push. Today I get to help others with some of their projects. Personal growth prepares us for what is coming.

I never spoke before thousands until I spoke before dozens. There is a process and a time and season to everything.

"To everything there is a season, a time for every purpose under heaven:"   —Ecclesiastes 3:1

My pastor always says, "If you hang around dogs you catch the fleas." It is the same with us. The people we surround ourselves with will tell a lot about not only where we are but where we are going. The morning I walked into the Green Room, I had no idea I'd partner with this great man. I was just excited about my day and my opportunity to speak into the lives of hundreds of pastors.

I was just a boy around 8 years old and I ordered a box of seeds from the back of a magazine to sell and make some extra money. We lived in Jacksonville Florida and I had no experience in farming but I was excited to sell seeds. I planted one corn seed in the yard and waited what seemed forever to get my crop of corn. Once the stock grew tall and the ear large I picked it and shook the ear of corn but the kernels were small and discolored. I later learned that you can't plant a single seed and expect it to grow to its full potential. Without cross pollination there's no way maturity can be reached. Without you and I cross pollinating with other leaders and entrepreneurs we will never mature and develop to our potential either. The cross pollination is part of the process. You and I are designed to learn from others, to be mentored and to mentor others.

It's time to ask yourself what you have to be excited about. Do you have an idea that God put into your heart? That definitely should excite you. Do you have a job, a family and your health? I know people who don't and they would gladly trade all their money for your life. You can find something to get excited about.

Busyness and effectiveness are 2 different things. Action and progress are not synonymous. Being mentored not only keeps you growing, but should also keep you doing the right thing for your life. Don't lose years doing unproductive things. You know what charges you up, and you know what you dread that takes the creative life right out of you.

One of the Nazis' methods of torture was to have the prisoners in the death camps do menial tasks over and over again until some chose to be shot to death rather than continue to do useless tasks. A rut is nothing more than a grave or a trench.

I think what makes a rut so hard to get out of is because you can't see your way out of it.

I have learned that when you're not pursuing your God-given destiny, you open yourself up to so many negative influences. Even the disciples of Jesus got negative, competitive and intolerant when they weren't chasing their mission. Let's take a look at Luke 9:46:

> *"Then a dispute arose among them as to which of them would be greatest."*

I like what Andrew Wommack says, "If you're all wrapped up in yourself you make a pretty small package." The disciples starting arguing amongst each other over who was the greatest in their group. That's astounding. Pursuing God's will for your life is not only a great decision but it will keep you focused on the needs of others. Solitude with no service to others makes you selfish. Jesus wanted to be alone quite often, but the needs of others compelled Him to stop and serve others (Matthew 14:14). Max Lucado tells a story about their annual family fishing trip. One year it was only Max and his father that could make the fishing trip. So Max's father told him he could invite a friend. Max and his friend were excited about the fishing trip and made plans. So they pulled up to the lake, set up the campsite and waited 'til morning to fish. But it rained that night and the next day so they couldn't fish. They read a few books, they played board games and waited for the rain to subside.

That evening a cold front moved in and froze the camper door shut. So another day was shot because of the weather. By the second day Max began to see some flaws in his friend he never noticed before and they started to pick on one another. You know what happened next day? The same thing happened, the weather kept them from fishing again, and the tension got worse between the boys. Finally Max's dad decided to break camp and just go home. The point of Max's story is this: when fishermen don't fish, they fight each other. You know how to stop conflict in your life? Get back to your mission. Help others and keep growing. When you have some solitude and you continue to serve others, you gain perspective in life. There are times to be alone, and there are times to grow and serve. Balance is power! If you're called to fish, fish and you'll flourish. Having a mentor will help you keep things in perspective, and as you mentor others, you help them. Having a mentor keeps you balanced in life. Commit to finding a mentor. A mentor can be anyone that has the ability to speak into your life. They don't have to live in your same hometown! You can certainly have mentors that are long distance, so long as you continue to listen, and educate yourself in their teachings.

Jesus made a statement in Mathew 12:30 Message translation:

"...if you're not helping, you're making things worse."

If you're mentoring, you're helping. Your own personal growth can be such a dynamic vehicle to propel you forward into your destiny. I promise if you take a passive lukewarm approach to finding and being a mentor, your chances are slim. Achievement starts with a decision.

"...I have set before you life and death, blessing and cursing; therefore choose life, that both you and your descendants may live."   —Deuteronomy 30:19

So it is our choice today whom we will serve. You can choose to follow God's plan for your life, or follow someone else's plan!

Our future and our destiny come one day at a time. Mentors and mentoring help us maximize those days. We must learn the value of a dream, a vision and a destiny to propel us through life. Mentors model many characteristics of success. Nothing can be more important in mentoring than modeling a vision of where you want to be.

OUR FUTURE AND OUR DESTINY COME ONE DAY AT A TIME!

There is a scripture in Genesis 1:29, *"And God said, 'See, I have given you every herb that yields seed which is on the face of all the earth, and every tree whose fruit yields seed; to you it shall be for food.'"* and Numbers 13:18, *"and see what the land is like: whether the people who dwell in it are strong or weak, few or many"*.

We must train ourselves to see things others don't see. We need to see opportunities, advantages and pitfalls. Mentors help you see what might go unnoticed by others. Recently I was in a Green Room full of influential people. Everyone was chatting and networking. Most of the time I would have been doing the same thing. But I saw someone sitting alone staring into a room full of people. I walked over and introduced myself and asked what his name was and where he was from. He told me his name and he began to tell me about his dilemma at home. It was sink or swim for him. It was almost a life or death situation with his business and family. Forty percent of businesses fail because of one crisis. As I listened it became clear what he should do. I realized that he knew what he needed to do but it was tough to make a decision that would potentially cost a million dollars and maybe the respect of his entire family and peers. At times doing the right thing can be harder than doing the wrong thing. But as one person put it "there's never a right time to do the wrong thing".

Sometimes a perfect stranger can clarify a tough decision for you. This man made the right choice that day and although it could have cost him a million dollars, it probably saved his family.

Mentors teach us in many areas of life to see the land for what it is and not what we fantasize it to be.

The Bible talks about mentoring more than you might think. The words disciple and disciplined followers are used hundreds of times in the Bible. Words like goal, vision, destiny and desire are used many times also. In fact, Paul was definitely a mentor and always used these principles when training others for the Master's use.

"And the things that you have heard from me among many witnesses, commit these to faithful men who will be able to teach others also."   —2 Timothy 2:2,

"Imitate me, just as I also imitate Christ."
                                                                 —1 Corinthians 11:1

You may have a dream but without a mentor you're like that one corn stock never to cross pollinate with others. Your chances of maximizing your dream are pretty slim.

Being mentored is for both you and the one mentoring you. You'll learn a lot about yourself, good, bad and ugly but it's worth it. Don't be one of those that talks only about what could have been, should have been and might have been. Go the extra mile and choose growth by following one that has been there before and succeeded.

* *

THE KEEP IT SIMPLE MENTALITY IS BE A MENTOR, HAVE A MENTOR!

6

STAY HUMBLE

What everyone reading this book is trying to do is win at Life. Happy people are humble people. Humility and poverty are not synonymous. Being financially or morally bankrupt is not humility.

"It is what you learn after you know it all that really counts"
—Coach John Wooden

My Pastor used to say, "The way up is the way down." If we were to build a building called "staying humble" you'd need a blueprint. A blueprint is produced and drawn up by engineers so the building can be built and if necessary duplicated. James 4:6 says,

"God resists the proud, But gives grace to the humble."

God resists the proud, and none of us want to be resisted by God, so let's create a "blueprint" on how to stay humble. The great thing about a blueprint is that if followed, you can repeat the results over and over again.

The bible is more that a literary work set in historical perspective. It's inspired by God and we can get our plan right from the inspired Word of God. To walk in any biblical truth we must be disciplined enough to follow the plan. Because God never fails, He has a plan and if we follow His plan to stay humble we won't ever have to be tripped up with pride or haughtiness. Pride will eventually bring you down and leave you powerless.

"And whoever exalts himself will be humbled, and he who humbles himself will be exalted." —Matthew 23:12

Pride is a deception from the enemy that we can and should live out of our own strength, wisdom, or resources. Pride will bring you down as fast as anything I know! Let's follow God's plan and build on an unshakeable foundation. It says in Luke 14:28-32 that when we embark on a project we need to first "count the cost." Counting the cost involves discovery on whether we first have the strength and resources to follow through with our plans all the way to completion. The reason why so many people fail in life is because they don't first have a plan to win. They have not taken the time to count the cost. Pride is an ugly thing that must be resisted. Pride says that you are all you need in this life. We've all seen people that have enjoyed some success, only to fall into the trap of self-dependence, and self-sufficiency. God never wants us to get to the point where we don't need, or seek Him anymore. I don't know about you but I don't want to get to the point where God is resisting me because I think I'm all that and a bag of chips! Anyone that is determined to stay humble even when they achieve success has to have the right perspective. Remind yourself daily Galatians 2:20:

"it is no longer I who live, but Christ lives in me."

When you carry that perspective that Christ lives in you and that He will never leave you, Hebrews 13:15: *"I will never leave you nor forsake you,"* you may not be starting your life with much but with God and His wisdom you can accomplish much. God will supply your every need to have a full life. You may be lacking in a lot of things but God is the master at filling in the gaps.

Build your new life with passion! When you pursue the right things with the right attitude, you can accomplish anything. Keep faith, family, friends, and finances high on your list of priorities and stay humble. If you do this, staying humble will be easy.

Keep a good consistent prayer life reminding yourself daily that God is first. When you have a blueprint you can follow, follow it again and again.

Never forget the lessons you learned on the way up. If you do, you will have re-learn them on the way back down. You see, the lessons or truths you learn when you have nothing, or when you are recovering from a broken relationship or some other setback, are the very foundation you build your future on.

When the tragedy of September 11, 2001 occurred and both Twin Towers crumpled, people were amazed that the piles of rubble were not hundreds of feet high. The towers were one hundred and ten stories. Thirteen hundred and sixty-eight feet high. Yet the skyscrapers that collapsed didn't leave piles of rubble hundreds of feet above the surface. We learned that the basement of the Towers went deep into the ground and then into the bedrock. So the buildings collapsed into the deep basement. In order to build these monumental buildings, they first had to dig down deep into the ground.

EVERY PERSON WHO YOU MEET KNOWS
SOMETHING YOU DON'T, SO LEARN FROM THEM
—H. JACKSON BROWN JR.

The foundation is as important as any other part of the building and is even more important when it comes to safety and stability. Life is the same way. The more our lives grow up the deeper we must grow down.

Never forget the lessons you learn as God teaches you principles of a healthy life.

"Humble yourself under the mighty hand of God..."

—1 Peter 5:6.

When I read the words "stay humble" on the newly acquired legal page from my friend, I thought a lot about it and asked him for his definition of what these simple words meant. During that conversation in his office, he said, "Let's get in the car, I want to take you somewhere."

We drove to Front Street along the water. As he stopped his luxury vehicle, he pointed to the large cruise ships docked at the big concrete port and stated, "I learned a lot about humility by losing that deal right there. That piece of land could have been mine but I didn't stay humble. I could have been making hundreds of thousands of dollars a month for the past thirty years and well into my future for only a fraction of what it is worth now."

He went on to explain. "If I had only been humble enough to keep my mouth shut. You see, an opportunity came up to purchase the land and I made a verbal deal to do so. I went and had breakfast with a few of my friends and was telling them about the deal. I spoke loudly and freely about the money I'd make with ships and tourists coming to the island. Unfortunately, a stranger at a table nearby went right to the land, got the number off the sign and offered a better deal if they would go to contract immediately."

"So you see, Dan," he concluded. "That is why I take you here today. So you can see the results of a lack of humility. Every time I see tourists walking down off those ships, I relive a very hard lesson."

He then offered this advice. "Learn it once and live it or it will cost you dearly."

LEARN IT ONCE AND LIVE IT!

I remember when I was in Bible School and Brother Kenneth Hagin would say that there are three things that bring preachers down.

- When they forget the lesson of humility.
- When they allow pride to take root.
- When they allow money and women to cloud their vision.

It is not how we start in life but how we finish!

* * * *

IT'S NOT HOW YOU START IN LIFE,
BUT HOW YOU FINISH!

* * * *

The Bible is filled with examples of people who first needed to make small adjustments in their thinking to gain insight and miracles. Little hinges open big doors Hurricane Carter said. The day we realize we don't know it all or that our way isn't the only way is not only humbling but liberating.

How many things are truly holding you back that you believe to be true although you haven't even considered other options? And, is it because you've not become humble enough to admit there may be another way?

J.M. Barrie, the creator of Peter Pan said, "Life is a long lesson in humility." I believe that and the sooner we learn that lesson, the sooner life becomes more manageable. Bad habits are holding many of us back. It is important to realize that even a broken clock is right twice a day. We train ourselves subconsciously to repeat bad habits or poor decision making and then call it the will of God. What is holding you back today from starting to get healthier, wealthier and wiser? What is stopping you from going on line and finding a seminar or conference you can attend that will start helping you?

History is going to keep repeating itself until we interrupt the process of our thinking. My personal definition of humility is having the right estimation of yourself. A lack of humility will bury us in mediocrity. A man in the Bible was blind and was on the side of the road begging. He had built an infrastructure around himself to be able to survive with his condition. In those days, they didn't have Social Security and Disability but what they did have was a garment you could wear that gave you the ability to beg for loose change from passers by.

> *"Now they came to Jericho. As He went out of Jericho with His disciples and a great multitude, blind Bartimaeus, the son of Timaeus, sat by the road begging. And when he heard that it was Jesus of Nazareth, he began to cry out and say, 'Jesus, Son of David, have mercy on me!'"* —Mark 10:46-47

The man had adapted himself to his disability and was convinced he would have to be blind the rest of his life so he was settling in for the long haul. He must have heard people talk about Jesus and His miracles as they passed by the roadside. Many times the blind and disabled would go to the road intersections to get in front of as many people as possible. Even after hearing about Jesus and His miracles, this man had to be humble enough to break his way of thinking about being blind for the rest of his life. It was that small glimmer of believing that began his possibility thinking, yet it was his willingness to be humble enough to admit his way was not the only way that brought about the change he needed to take the action to receive his healing.

> *"And throwing aside his garment, he rose and came to Jesus."*   —Mark 10:50

He threw off the very garment that gave him the legal right to beg. You must realize that when a blind man throws off his garment, the chance of him finding it again is slim. He had a change of thinking that led to a change of life. You know there were nefarious people who would have picked that coat as soon as he dropped it and swindled people out of money.

> *"And throwing aside his garment, he rose and came to Jesus. So Jesus answered and said to him, 'What do you want Me to do for you?' The blind man said to Him, 'Rabboni, that I may receive my sight.' Then Jesus said to him, 'Go your way;*

your faith has made you well.' And immediately he received his sight and followed Jesus on the road."

—Matthew 10:50-52

Humbling yourself is mostly about where you put your attention. Humility is not thinking less of yourself, but thinking less about yourself. This ultimately leaves room for God's opportunities in your life and your corresponding actions to dominate you. When God's Word states that you are healed and blessed, or that you are an overcomer and you choose to believe, that is what sparks the changes in your thinking.

HUMILITY IS NOT THINKING LESS OF YOURSELF BUT THINKING LESS ABOUT YOURSELF!

False humility can take on a lot of faces. It is a good lesson to learn not to merely go through the motions of Christianity but to really believe what God says about you.

"Most assuredly, I say to you, he who believes in Me, the works that I do he will do also; and greater works than these he will do, because I go to My Father. And whatever you ask in My name, that I will do, that the Father may be glorified in the Son. If you ask anything in My name, I will do it."

—John 14:12-14

These words are the color red in my Bible. That means they were the very words Jesus spoke. He said the works He did you will do and greater works. False humility winces back and says, 'I could never pray and heal someone or I could never really make a difference in the world.' But, that is not how the Bible defines humility; that is total unbelief. The keep it simple mentality is just so simple. Just believe what God says about you. That's true humility.

Take God's Word seriously! In fact, believe it as much as if you would receive it from a doctor, lawyer or trusted family member.

If you would act on a lawyer's word, how much more should you act on God's Word? About 25 years ago, I remember entering into a real estate deal and someone got a lawyer involved. I had never had to deal with a lawyer or judge before and, to say the least, I was nervous. In fact, I was so nervous that it was affecting my sleep and peace of mind.

A businessman in the church had me meet him at his lawyer's office to explain our problem. The attorney asked me if I had two thousand dollars. Once I answered yes, he told me to write a check which I did and then I gave it to him. He then said, "Now you just paid me to worry for you so stop worrying."

The funny thing is I really believed him and I didn't worry about the case anymore. It was no big deal and it just worked out exactly like the attorney said it would. I learned so much about humility in that situation. I learned that if I can believe an attorney about a case and its favorable outcome, how much more can I trust God who loves me and wants the best for me. I learned that I can trust the God who promised that He would never leave me or forsake me.

"I will never leave you nor forsake you." —Hebrews 13:5(b),

The Bible teaches us to cast our cares on the Lord.

"Therefore humble yourselves under the mighty hand of God, that He may exalt you in due time, casting all your care upon Him, for He cares for you. Be sober, be vigilant; because your adversary the devil walks about like a roaring lion, seeking whom he may devour." —1Peter 5:6-8

All my worries, anxieties and woes didn't amount to a hill of beans. God promised me that He would deliver me from all evil.

"If we confess our sins, He is faithful and just to forgive us our sins and to cleanse us from all unrighteousness." —1 John 1:9

Bible humility is about having a change in our priorities. We choose to believe what God says about us. It is time to see things differently. You are neither born a winner or loser. You are born chooser!

YOU ARE A BORN CHOOSER!

"And Elijah came to all the people, and said, 'How long will you falter between two opinions? If the Lord is God, follow Him; but if Baal, follow him.'" —1 Kings 18:21(a)

What a powerful chapter on true humility. This chapter illustrates total dependence on God in the face of overwhelming odds in the natural.

"but the people who know their God shall be strong, and carry out great exploits." —Daniel 11:32(b)

What are you faced with today? Is it a bad diagnosis from the doctor? Or, is it bad news from a banker or an attorney? Maybe the odds are even totally against you, but you know your God so you will remain strong and do great exploits. You will be an example to others, not an excuse to fail. That is because God is more than enough to get you through your storm or your fiery furnace. He will make it so you won't get wet or even smell of smoke.

The absence of humility can reveal itself in a lack of trusting God or it could be downright arrogance. The center of all sin is "I." There is no getting around it. You set yourself up for a fall when you become the most important thing in your life. In other words, never dislocate your arm while patting yourself on the back. Have you ever noticed that the more you pat some people on the back, the bigger their head swells? I like what John Mason, author, says, "Even a postage stamp becomes useless when it gets stuck on itself."

Andrew Womack puts it this way, "When you get wrapped up in yourself, you make a pretty small package."

Norman Vincent Peale said, "The man who lives for himself is a failure."

According to Jesus in Matthew 20:25-28, *"But Jesus called them to Himself and said, 'You know that the rulers of the Gentiles lord it over them, and those who are great exercise authority over them. Yet it shall not be so among you; but whoever desires to become great among you, let him be your servant. And whoever desires to be first among you, let him be your slave—just as the Son of Man did not come to be served, but to serve, and to give His life a ransom for many.'"*

If ego has taken over your soul, chances are there are not too many people clamoring to be around you. No one wants to hear how great you think you are. It doesn't matter how you start, it's how you finish. So it is time to make some midcourse corrections and let go of your ego so you can finish strong and never blow your own horn again. Keep it simple and stay humble.

Face the fact that without Jesus we are all just a big hot mess. But, with Him, we can do all things He has called us to do. Keep it simple from now on. Humble yourselves and if God wants to exalt you so be it. And, let's help others realize their potential and serve them. After all, that is the only true way to be great in His Kingdom.

IF YOU WANT TO BE GREAT
YOU HAVE TO SERVE OTHERS!

I've heard a great deal about people working on their legacy, yet it doesn't line up with what the Bible says. I see a lot about building God's Kingdom and giving Him the glory for all He does through us as believers. If we're ever going to boast again, let us boast about the family we belong to and the God Who adopted us as His very own.

"just as He chose us in Him before the foundation of the world, that we should be holy and without blame before Him in love, having predestined us to adoption as sons by Jesus Christ to Himself, according to the good pleasure of His will, to the praise of the glory of His grace, by which He made us accepted in the Beloved." —Ephesians 1:4-6

Our true identity is in Christ and if we have received His attributes and the fruits of the Spirit are prevalent in our lives, then there won't be much room for our never satisfied ego.

WHEN CHRIST'S ATTRIBUTES AND THE FRUIT OF THE SPIRIT ARE PREVALENT IN OUR LIVES, THERE WON'T BE MUCH ROOM FOR OUR NEVER SATISFIED EGO!

"Therefore, if anyone is in Christ, he is a new creation; old things have passed away; behold, all things have become new." —2 Corinthians 5:17

I am a firm believer that this scripture should be part of all our testimonies.

"I have been crucified with Christ; it is no longer I who live, but Christ lives in me; and the life which I now live in the flesh I live by faith in the Son of God, who loved me and gave Himself for me." —Galatians 2:20

And the reality of Galatians that Paul alludes to should be ours as well. Saul died out there on that road the day Jesus spoke to him and he became a new man. Saul could boast of a pedigree that would put most to shame, yet he was lost, miserable and on his way to a Christless eternity. In fact, Saul died that day and Paul lived!

"Then Saul, still breathing threats and murder against the disciples of the Lord, went to the high priest and asked letters from him to the synagogues of Damascus, so that if

he found any who were of the Way, whether men or women, he might bring them bound to Jerusalem. As he journeyed he came near Damascus, and suddenly a light shone around him from heaven. Then he fell to the ground, and heard a voice saying to him, 'Saul, Saul, why are you persecuting Me?' And he said, 'Who are You, Lord?' Then the Lord said, 'I am Jesus, whom you are persecuting. It is hard for you to kick against the goads.' So he, trembling and astonished, said, 'Lord, what do You want me to do?' Then the Lord said to him, 'Arise and go into the city, and you will be told what you must do.'" —Acts 9:1-6

There was no longer room for Saul's pedigree, education and résumé where he was going.

"Now there was a certain disciple at Damascus named Ananias; and to him the Lord said in a vision, 'Ananias.' And he said, 'Here I am, Lord.' So the Lord said to him, 'Arise and go to the street called Straight, and inquire at the house of Judas for one called Saul of Tarsus, for behold, he is praying. And in a vision he has seen a man named Ananias coming in and putting his hand on him, so that he might receive his sight.' Then Ananias answered, 'Lord, I have heard from many about this man, how much harm he has done to Your saints in Jerusalem. And here he has authority from the chief priests to bind all who call on Your name.' But the Lord said to him, 'Go, for he is a chosen vessel of Mine to bear My name before Gentiles, kings, and the children of Israel. For I will show him how many things he must suffer for My name's sake.' And Ananias went his way and entered the house; and laying his hands on him he said, 'Brother Saul, the Lord Jesus, who appeared to you on the road as you came, has sent me that you may receive your sight and be filled with the Holy Spirit.' Immediately there fell from his eyes something like scales, and he received his sight at once; and he arose and was baptized." —Acts 9:10-18

When Christ fills you on the inside, there is not much room for self. Don't let the flesh and self, crawl back up to get in the way of your progress. You're a new creature just like Paul. The past is the past. Let it go! Keep it simple and let the old you stay dead while allowing God's light to shine through you. The new you looks so much better!

The Past Is The Past, Let It Go!

THE PAST IS THE PAST, LET IT GO!

"Immediately he preached the Christ in the synagogues, that He is the Son of God."   —Acts 9:20

THE KEEP IT SIMPLE MENTALITY IS STAY HUMBLE!

7

SOMEBODY UP THERE LIKES ME

After a week of being with my new friend, my comfort level was such that I had no problem asking him many different questions about his family, hobbies, friends and even his dislikes. He usually would redirect me towards the business at hand like setting up the logistics and preparing for the upcoming event.

Finally I asked him point blank what he meant when he wrote on that now infamous page that "Somebody up there likes me". He gave out a loud belly laugh and said, "It is the little things in life that will mean the most to you as you grow older!"

He continued, "I had to learned personally that God loves me and that He cares for me, knows everything about me and still loves me. You don't find that in many humans."

He looked intently into my eyes and spoke these profound words, "Most people love conditionally, but God loves me, warts and all, the good, bad and ugly. Dan, I've learned there is only one perfect person that ever walked this planet and there will only ever be one. And, since God loves me, I learned that I ought to start loving myself."

His story got a little more personal. "You see Dan, I had a vice in my life that almost killed me. It all started because I thought since I was an orphan that nobody loved me. Even though I was successful in many areas of life, I had a huge blind spot when it came to my self-worth. God had to show me He loved me and He did it through a very special way.

"Success, whether it is business, political or any other area, can never make up for the eight-foot gorilla in the corner of the room called self. You live with yourself twenty-four hours a day. I really didn't like me since I was convinced no one wanted me as a child. God had to make John 3:16 a reality for me and that He had a plan for my life (Jeremiah 29:11). Once these were settled within me, I could then allow His favor in my life to promote me in every area!"

"For God so loved the world that He gave His only begotten Son, that whoever believes in Him should not perish but have everlasting life." —John 3:16

"For I know the thoughts that I think toward you, says the Lord, thoughts of peace and not of evil, to give you a future and a hope." —Jeremiah 29:11

At that point I asked him to define favor for me. He answered, "In sports, playing a match or game on your home field with your own fans is an advantage."

"Well," he continued, "God's on your side and, with His favor, the game is fixed to your advantage. God brings the right people into your life and brings the right business or job and opportunities too."

He then went on to explain, "See, people are like elevators. Some take you up and some take you down. You'll be surprised, Dan, how well your life will go when you get the wrong people out of your life. In fact, God's favor will help you always make the playing field a home field advantage."

PEOPLE ARE LIKE ELEVATORS, SOME TAKE YOU UP AND SOME TAKE YOU DOWN!

Favor is an advantage we can have in every area of life and you can count on God's help.

"And Jesus increased in wisdom and stature, and in favor with God and men." —Luke 2:52

Belonging to God has distinct advantages that only come by relationship.

"May the Lord God of your fathers make you a thousand times more numerous than you are, and bless you as He has promised you!" —Deuteronomy 1:11

Favor and faithfulness are closely connected. When you're connected to God through His Word, His church and an intimate relationship, you have favor, the home field advantage. Where did this favor start for you and me? It started in the beginning.

"Then God blessed them, and God said to them, 'Be fruitful and multiply; fill the earth and subdue it; have dominion over the fish of the sea, over the birds of the air, and over every living thing that moves on the earth.'" —Genesis 1:28

God blessed original man and has never stopped since. The only thing that can separate you from His favor is for you to reject Him and His love for you. If you are a believer, you're part of God's family and He plays favorites for His kids.

"For thus says the Lord of hosts: 'He sent Me after glory, to the nations which plunder you; for he who touches you touches the apple of His eye.'" —Zechariah 2:8

"But now, thus says the Lord, who created you, O Jacob, and He who formed you, O Israel: 'Fear not, for I have redeemed you; I have called you by your name; You are Mine. When you pass through the waters, I will be with you; and through the rivers, they shall not overflow you. When you walk through the fire, you shall not be burned, nor shall the flame scorch you.'" —Isaiah 43:1-2

My siblings and I were raised by a father who had abandonment issues. He never knew his father and his mother gave him up, so he learned that he was not loved and not wanted, valued, or esteemed. You can imagine what that does to a child. He was passed from relative to relative, whoever could afford to keep him during depression days. He definitely had issues showing love and getting close to people. He never really had any close friends. I know he had no lifelong friends. Even his relationship with God seemed distant and impersonal by the type of church he chose to attend, and that we were raised in. It wasn't until he retired that he let his guard down a little and let people in a little. Even his relationship with God seemed to strengthen after he retired.

He felt he was unloved and it wasn't until he slowed down that he began to realize that somebody up there liked him. I never wanted to live my life without real friends. I really sought God about His love for me personally and in every supernatural way He showed me, and many of my brothers and sisters that God does indeed love us. The Lord spoke to me personally during a very trying time in my life and told me, "No matter who else does in life, I will never leave you nor forsake you."

I have seen over and over again that true-life transformation happens when anyone realizes we are valuable and God does love us. When someone loves you and you love them, things change in dynamic ways. Think of your children (if you have children!), or of someone you love. If it was in your power to fix a problem they had, you would do so because of your love for them. Regardless the cost, you would lay down your life for your child or loved one. That comes from love. With your husband or wife it's the exact same thing. I know of a man whose daughter needed a kidney. The father was tested and he was found to be a match for his beautiful daughter. It wasn't but few days and a kidney was removed from the father and transferred to the daughter preserving her life. She never lost a minute of sleep the rest of her life wondering if her father loved her. I also know of a Pastor that needed a kidney. Someone from his congregation was a perfect match and she gave her Pastor the gift of one of her kidneys. He never wondered whether this church member really loved her Pastor.

Once a person knows how much God loves them it changes everything. Jesus laid down His life for us because He loves us (John 15:13). He loves us so much He sent the Holy Spirit to lead us and guide us into all the truth (John 14:26). We should have no abandonment issues because someone up the likes us and God Himself has even sent us the Helper to fill us, lead us, guide us into the truth.

As I reflect over past years in my life, I can see God's favor because I have a praying mother. My mom took me in her arms when I was a toddler and prayed, "Lord, make him a Priest." Although my mom was disappointed that I did not go into the "Priesthood," she eventually understood that my becoming a Pastor and Minister were one and the same.

If you look back over your life, you can probably see God's fingerprints all over the place. If you rejected God, you can probably see the devil's hands at work trying to kill you and destroy your future with drugs, violence or some other tactic.

"The thief does not come except to steal, and to kill, and to destroy." —John 10:10(a)

Following God and choosing His ways are like a magnet when it comes to attracting divine favor.

"Now therefore, listen to me, my children, for blessed are those who keep my ways. Hear instruction and be wise, and do not disdain it. Blessed is the man who listens to me, watching daily at my gates, Waiting at the posts of my doors. For whoever finds me finds life, and obtains favor from the Lord;" —Proverbs 8:32-35

Listening to my politically and financially successful friend made me want to know more about his kind of favor. At that time of my life, I had more excuses than I had favor and I liked his definition better than mine. I rehearsed in my mind that here was an orphan child who was successfully navigating life almost by himself and had figured out that somebody up there really did like him.

I, on the other hand, was still struggling over some of these issues and never grew up with half the obstacles he had. I was at least wise enough to listen intently as he spoke about the favor of God. He told me that once I found out about the favor God has for all His children, it was important to tell someone else about it. So that night, I decided to do just that and determined to tell someone else about God's love and favor for all His children.

During this trip, one of my responsibilities was to speak in churches and schools as well as the media. I was speaking at a church that evening and as I talked about God's favor, I could see the light go on in the faces of those at the church. The revelation that God was not mad at anyone and that He loved them and wanted to help them in life brought about an atmosphere of hope and expectation throughout the congregation.

My text was gleaned from Proverbs, Ephesians and the Gospel of John. I asked who had been blessed with all spiritual blessing in Christ?

> *"Blessed be the God and Father of our Lord Jesus Christ, who has blessed us with every spiritual blessing in the heavenly places in Christ,"* —Ephesians 1:3

I encouraged them that we have been purchased and redeemed.

> *"In Him we have redemption through His blood, the forgiveness of sins, according to the riches of His grace which He made to abound toward us in all wisdom and prudence,"* —Ephesians 1:7-8

"But he who is joined to the Lord is one spirit with Him."

—1 Corinthians 6:17

"For you were bought at a price; therefore glorify God in your body and in your spirit, which are God's."

—1 Corinthians 6:20

I talked about the financial prosperity that comes as well as forgiveness of sin.

"I love those who love me, and those who seek me find me. With me are riches and honor, enduring wealth and prosperity. My fruit is better than fine gold; what I yield surpasses choice silver. I walk in the way of righteousness, along the paths of justice, bestowing a rich inheritance on those who love me and making their treasuries full."

—Proverbs 8:17-21(NIV)

"If we confess our sins, He is faithful and just to forgive us our sins and to cleanse us from all unrighteousness."

—1 John 1:9

It was quite a night!

Getting back to my lessons. My friend talked about all the gifts and talents God gives to His children as He determines.

"Therefore He says: 'When He ascended on high, He led captivity captive, And gave gifts to men.'" —Ephesians 4:8

"Having then gifts differing according to the grace that is given to us, let us use them:" —Romans 12:6(a)

It reminded me of something that happened to me as a young boy. I had a friend, Bart, whose dad was a team doctor at the University of Florida. Hanging out with Bart definitely had its perks. Not only were we classmates, but we were friends and his dad was able to get us into the University of Florida basketball games free. We were even able to get close and personal with the team players.

During the early seventies, LSU was playing the University of Florida. LSU's star player was a young man named Peter Maravich, better known by his nickname, Pistol Pete. Pistol Pete was the Michael Jordan or LeBron James of his time. He was the man. I was fortunate enough go with Bart's family to the basketball game a few hours early and went to the field house. Most of the lights were off and just a few people were milling around. I walked out of the player's training room to the huge stadium. I was all alone sitting on one of the floor level seats right next to one of the baskets.

I could hear noise coming from the visitor locker room so I knew LSU was in the house. After several minutes, I heard a single basketball being dribbled down the hall leading from the locker room to the field house. Then, as big as life, there he was all by himself, Pistol Peter Maravich. He was dribbling a ball and got out on the floor before all the lights were turned on. He just kept dribbling and shooting real close to the basket. Then he would back up a step and repeat the process. Again and again he shot the ball and kept backing up. He was out there more than thirty minutes before any other player came out.

Pistol Pete was the best on the court in all of college basketball and he was also the first at practice. So you see, even when God gives us a talent, it has to be developed and honed. Pete knew his best effort at practice was the key to having his God given talent the best chance to flourish. His talent in basketball was one of the avenues God was able to show him favor. Pistol Pete eventually signed the first million-dollar contract in the NBA. He and I had a special moment there after his warm up that no one else got to have. Why? Because I was the early bird also that day. Anyone could have joined us but no one did. No lights, no cameras, no press, just a little boy and a super star ball player. I learned a lot that day. Someone up there likes me too. He had me in the right place at the right time for me to meet one of my heroes.

Your God given talent and desires will open doors of favor for you. God's favor in your life changes everything. We live and operate in a predominately secular world that ignores or rebels against God. Don't tell me you don't need favor. I ask God for favor all the time.

YOUR GOD GIVEN TALENT AND DESIRES WILL OPEN DOORS OF FAVOR FOR YOU!

Dealing with a secular world, we need the favor of God as a Christian. In fact, in this secular environment we now live, believers are labeled right wing extremists. Throughout the Bible believers have been persecuted and today the same thing is happening. We are going through it today and as time goes on, it will be getting worse and worse. Today believers are being killed for their faith. Satan has no new tricks. He's come to kill steal, kill and destroy.

Joseph, the youngest son of Jacob (Israel), had favor being the youngest. He got a coat of many colors which brought him favor from his father and was despised by his brothers.

"Now Israel loved Joseph more than all his children, because he was the son of his old age. Also he made him a tunic of many colors. But when his brothers saw that their father loved him more than all his brothers, they hated him and could not speak peaceably to him." —Genesis 37:3-4

Having God's favor doesn't mean you will never have another problem, it merely means you and God will overcome any problem because somebody up there loves you.

HAVING GOD'S FAVOR MEANS YOU AND GOD WILL OVERCOME ANY PROBLEM YOU FACE!

I remember calling my dad one day when I was at a give up point in my life. Some of the people in the church were really putting undue pressure on me that they would never have put on themselves. I was attempting to do ministry in my own strength and my dad had to explain to me that as long as I dealt with life I'd have to deal with people. He told me that people are always the problem and they are always the solution. He was right!

PEOPLE ARE ALWAYS THE PROBLEM AND THEY ARE ALWAYS THE SOLUTION!

Joseph was thrown into a pit and sold into slavery by his own brothers. I've been in some disagreements with my brothers but we never threw each other into a pit to be sold as a slave. That is a level of dysfunction only Dr. Phil can deal with. Their jealousy and anger was so fierce that at first they were contemplating killing Joseph.

> *"Now when they saw him afar off, even before he came near them, they conspired against him to kill him. Then they said to one another, 'Look, this dreamer is coming! Come therefore, let us now kill him and cast him into some pit; and we shall say, "Some wild beast has devoured him." We shall see what will become of his dreams!'"* —Genesis 37:18-20

But, they were talked into selling him as a slave instead.

> *"'Come and let us sell him to the Ishmaelites, and let not our hand be upon him, for he is our brother and our flesh.' And his brothers listened. Then Midianite traders passed by; so the brothers pulled Joseph up and lifted him out of the pit, and sold him to the Ishmaelites for twenty shekels of silver. And they took Joseph to Egypt."* —Genesis 37:27-28

But, because of the favor of God, Joseph soon found himself working for Potiphar, Pharaoh's right hand man.

"The Lord was with Joseph, and he was a successful man; and he was in the house of his master the Egyptian. And his master saw that the Lord was with him and that the Lord made all he did to prosper in his hand. So Joseph found favor in his sight, and served him. Then he made him overseer of his house, and all that he had he put under his authority. So it was, from the time that he had made him overseer of his house and all that he had, that the Lord blessed the Egyptian's house for Joseph's sake; and the blessing of the Lord was on all that he had in the house and in the field. Thus he left all that he had in Joseph's hand, and he did not know what he had except for the bread which he ate. Now Joseph was handsome in form and appearance." —Genesis 29:2-6

Joseph didn't do what all the other prisoners did. Just like we can't do what poor people do. God's favor on Joseph's life caused him to prosper in everything he did. How we all would like that to be our testimony! Wouldn't it be nice if everywhere you went, everyone you met would talk about the fact that you have the golden touch? I was speaking at a large church not too long ago. A man walked up to me and said that the first time he set eyes on me, the Lord told him that I was a picture of prosperity. Whenever I see that man, he always retells me that story.

Joseph prospered in everything he did. (Pr.10:22 NIV) The blessing of the Lord brings wealth without painful toil. Potiphar's wife told some lies about Joseph and he wound up in jail. But jail didn't end up in him. He and his dream became bigger than jail (Genesis 37:6-10). Somebody up there liked Joseph. Remember, somebody up there likes you and has already given you their blessing and favor.

"Blessed be the God and Father of our Lord Jesus Christ, who has blessed us with every spiritual blessing in the heavenly places in Christ," —Ephesians 1:3

"I call heaven and earth as witnesses today against you, that I have set before you life and death, blessing and cursing; therefore choose life, that both you and your descendants may live; that you may love the Lord your God, that you may obey His voice, and that you may cling to Him, for He is your life and the length of your days; and that you may dwell in the land which the Lord swore to your fathers, to Abraham, Isaac, and Jacob, to give them." —Deuteronomy 30:19-20

Joseph was enslaved one day and the next he was promoted to the keeper of Potiphar's household. Why? Because somebody up there liked him.

"The Lord was with Joseph, so he succeeded in everything he did as he served in the home of his Egyptian master. Potiphar noticed this and realized that the Lord was with Joseph, giving him success in everything he did. This pleased Potiphar, so he soon made Joseph his personal attendant. He put him in charge of his entire household and everything he owned. From the day Joseph was put in charge of his master's household and property, the Lord began to bless Potiphar's household for Joseph's sake. All his household affairs ran smoothly, and his crops and livestock flourished. So Potiphar gave Joseph complete administrative responsibility over everything he owned." —Genesis 39:2-6

With Joseph there, he didn't worry about a thing—except what kind of food to eat!

Soon Potiphar's wife took a liking to him and accused him of trying to rape her.

"and Potiphar's wife soon began to look at him lustfully. 'Come and sleep with me,' she demanded.

But Joseph refused. 'Look,' he told her, 'my master trusts me with everything in his entire household. No one here has more authority than I do. He has held back nothing from me except you, because you are his wife. How could I do such a wicked thing? It would be a great sin against God.'

She kept putting pressure on Joseph day after day, but he refused to sleep with her, and he kept out of her way as much as possible. One day, however, no one else was around when he went in to do his work. She came and grabbed him by his cloak, demanding, 'Come on, sleep with me!' Joseph tore himself away, but he left his cloak in her hand as he ran from the house.

When she saw that she was holding his cloak and he had fled, she called out to her servants. Soon all the men came running. 'Look!' she said. 'My husband has brought this Hebrew slave here to make fools of us! He came into my room to rape me, but I screamed. When he heard me scream, he ran outside and got away, but he left his cloak behind with me.'

She kept the cloak with her until her husband came home."

—Genesis. 39:7-16

Maybe this doesn't look like favor on Joseph's life to you but God was with him!

I don't think you could possibly be in a worse place than Joseph was. He was abandoned by his family, sold into slavery, working as a servant and wrongly slandered. The unique trait about Joseph was that he set up a "no excuse zone," in his life.

● ● ● ●

JOSEPH SET UP A NO EXCUSE ZONE IN HIS LIFE!

● ● ● ●

You can have excuses or you can have results, but you can't have both. The father of Jacob was lied to by his own sons and he thought it was over for Jacob, yet we see that it was not. He had no idea that favor was working for him in his future. We can learn a lot from that alone! Even when we don't realize it, God's favor is working for us and blessing us.

While Joseph was in prison, the warden spotted him and the favor of God promoted him to the warden's right hand man. His life and station, even in prison, improved because of God's favor.

"Then Joseph's master took him and put him into the prison, a place where the king's prisoners were confined. And he was there in the prison. But the Lord was with Joseph and showed him mercy, and He gave him favor in the sight of the keeper of the prison. And the keeper of the prison committed to Joseph's hand all the prisoners who were in the prison; whatever they did there, it was his doing. The keeper of the prison did not look into anything that as under Joseph's authority, because the Lord was with him; and whatever he did, the Lord made it prosper." —Genesis 39:20-23

The Lord was with him and everything he did prospered even in prison.

THE LORD WAS WITH HIM AND EVERYTHING HE DID PROSPERED, EVEN IN PRISON!

Some of you who are reading this book are in prisons of guilt because of an abortion years ago. Maybe it was a failed marriage or a bankruptcy. The prisons are built to keep us there. Jesus came to set us free from prison walls that are really only in our minds. They tell us things like, 'you're not loved because you're orphaned,' or 'someone gave you up for adoption because you're not worthy.'

Others live in the prisons of their minds about being overweight or underpaid or even overlooked at the office for a promotion. God's favor on your life can break down the mental walls that have been built up.

Joseph's life included an opportunity to interpret the dream of the butler and baker who were imprisoned with him. In one day, everything in Joseph's life changed. Although it took a while for the favor of God to work for this interpreter of dreams because others forgot about the good Joseph had done for them, God did not. Remember, God is not a respecter of persons so if you've experienced similar situations, take comfort in knowing your time is coming. Somebody up there likes you.

> *"And they said to him, 'We each have had a dream, and there is no interpreter of it.' So Joseph said to them, 'Do not interpretations belong to God? Tell them to me, please.'"*
>
> —Genesis 40:8

> *"And Joseph said to him, 'This is the interpretation of it: The three branches are three days. Now within three days Pharaoh will lift up your head and restore you to your place, and you will put Pharaoh's cup in his hand according to the former manner, when you were his butler. But remember me when it is well with you, and please show kindness to me; make mention of me to Pharaoh, and get me out of this house.'"*
> —Genesis 40:12-14

> *"Then he restored the chief butler to his butlership again, and he placed the cup in Pharaoh's hand. But he hanged the chief baker, as Joseph had interpreted to them. Yet the chief butler did not remember Joseph, but forgot him."* —Genesis 40:21-23

Although it would seem that Joseph had been forgotten, God was still at work. Two years is a long time to be forgotten but if you keep your eyes on God, He will help you maximize the time.

> *"And we know that all things work together for good to those who love God, to those who are the called according to His purpose."*
> —Romans 8:28

To say the least, God didn't forget Joseph, which proves the statement, delay is not denial. It is not a perfect world we live in and that is why we need faith and favor.

"Who shall separate us from the love of Christ? Shall tribulation, or distress, or persecution, or famine, or nakedness, or peril, or sword?"   —Romans 8:35

"Yet in all these things we are more than conquerors through Him who loved us."   —Romans 8:37

IT IS NOT A PERFECT WORLD WE LIVE IN AND THAT IS WHY WE NEED FAITH AND FAVOR!

When God shows favor, it is evident to everyone. Pharaoh needed a dream interpreted and the butler suddenly got a conscience and remembered Joseph and his ability to interpret dreams.

"Now it came to pass in the morning that his spirit was troubled, and he sent and called for all the magicians of Egypt and all its wise men. And Pharaoh told them his dreams, but there was no one who could interpret them for Pharaoh. Then the chief butler spoke to Pharaoh, saying: 'I remember my faults this day.'"   —Genesis 41:8-9

The gift God had given Joseph brought favor and prosperity for him. The gift God had given Pistol Peter Maravich brought him favor and prosperity. The same is true for each and every one of you!

"Then Pharaoh sent and called Joseph, and they brought him quickly out of the dungeon; and he shaved, changed his clothing, and came to Pharaoh. And Pharaoh said to Joseph, 'I have had a dream, and there is no one who can interpret it. But I have heard it said of you that you can understand a dream, to interpret it.'"   —Genesis 41:14-15

Joseph arrived from the prison to the palace in no time. I believe this to be a word directly from the Lord for all those reading this. Your lives, businesses, marriages, connections and children can change overnight. God is truly the master at the change game and He brings favor to you which can and will change everything.

> *"This is the thing which I have spoken to Pharaoh. God has shown Pharaoh what He is about to do. Indeed seven years of great plenty will come throughout all the land of Egypt; but after them seven years of famine will arise, and all the plenty will be forgotten in the land of Egypt; and the famine will deplete the land. So the plenty will not be known in the land because of the famine following, for it will be very severe. And the dream was repeated to Pharaoh twice because the thing is established by God, and God will shortly bring it to pass. Now therefore, let Pharaoh select a discerning and wise man, and set him over the land of Egypt."*
>
> —Genesis 41:28-33

You may think God is late and you might think God has overlooked you or forgotten you but I am telling you that it is a set up because somebody up there likes you...even loves you! He's been working the whole time on your behalf, even when all you can see are prison walls or a whale's belly. Favor and prosperity can happen in one day.

> *"Then Pharaoh said to Joseph, 'Inasmuch as God has shown you all this, there is no one as discerning and wise as you. You shall be over my house, and all my people shall be ruled according to your word; only in regard to the throne will I be greater than you.' And Pharaoh said to Joseph, 'See, I have set you over all the land of Egypt.' Then Pharaoh took his signet ring off his hand and put it on Joseph's hand; and he clothed him in garments of fine linen and put a gold chain around his neck. And he had him ride in the second chariot which he had; and they cried out before him, 'Bow the knee!' So he set him over all the land of Egypt."*
>
> —Genesis 41:39-43

I know many have been waiting a long time. I want to encourage you today to stop waiting and start preparing for the walls to come down so you can walk out with your head held high. Promotion is right around the corner for many of you. In fact, repeat ten times, "Somebody up there likes me!!!"

• •

THE KEEP IT SIMPLE SOMEBODY MENTALITY IS KNOWING SOMEBODY UP THERE LIKES ME!

8

THE NO EXCUSE ZONE

As my time on the island was winding down, I was able to have a final meal with my friend. I knew this would probably be my last alone time with him since the whole team of well over a hundred people would be flying to the island in the morning. I thanked him for all his time and help with navigation through the land mines of the local civic establishment. I also thanked him for all the phone calls he made in order to make our job seamless.

I also wanted to talk to him about an entry he had made on the legal page he had given me that first day we met. It was a one liner on the back side of the page towards the bottom, circled, underlined in red several times and highlighted in yellow. So, I asked him what he meant by, 'Make your life a no excuse zone.'

He gave his familiar laugh out loud response and said, "Dan, in life you can have excuses or you can have results but you can't have both." He then quoted A. R. Bernard, Evangelist, Spiritual Leader, CEO, Senior Advisor, Television Personality, Author, Motivational Speaker, and Life Coach who put it this way. "Excuses are the crutches of the uncommitted."

YOU CAN HAVE EXCUSES OR YOU CAN
HAVE RESULTS, BUT YOU CAN'T HAVE BOTH!

My friend went on to tell me, "People who have excuses usually don't have much of anything else. Never give yourself the luxury of quitting. Don't leave a backdoor open just in case things don't work out. It is said that Cortez, once they reached the new world burned their ships. As a result his men were well motivated and committed to building a future. Don't quit, don't give up. I never have because there is no future in it. Nobody remembers who came in second, heck, they only remember the winner for a minute, so do what you do for the right reasons."

"Everyone knows Alexander Graham Bell invented the telephone but what most people don't know is a German inventor named Philip Reis came real close to inventing the phone before Bell. The Reis Machine could do everything except communicate the human voice and only transmitted static, humming and whistles.

Reis gave up on the invention too soon. Bell took his invention several years later, adjusted a small screw one-thousandth of an inch to control the electrodes and he had a working telephone."

Reis was within one-thousandth of an inch.

My friend concluded, "Dan, think about it, a mere one-thousandth of an inch separated Reis from being known as the person who invented such a marvelous tool for communication."

So you see, you can have excuses or you can have results, but you can't have both. Keep your life simple and make it a no excuse zone. If something is worth starting, it is worth finishing. Can you imagine being as close as one-thousandth of an inch away from your goal and giving up? Yet people do it all the time. They just don't know it.

* * * * *

IF SOMETHING IS WORTH STARTING,
IT IS WORTH FINISHING!

* * * *

Here is a good key to life that can help you succeed. You never know how close you are to your breakthrough. Throughout life, we're all going to have to make small adjustments. Someone is going to have to pay the price to start the ball rolling in anything.

He then told me, "My success has not only changed me but my whole generation. I struggled and made adjustments so others could benefit also. I have scores of employees who have been with me for years and whose lives are much better off because of adjustments I've had to make. In fact, it was Edward Judson who said, 'If you succeed without suffering, it is because someone else has suffered before you.'"

His wisdom was mesmerizing. "Dan, if you suffer without succeeding it is that someone else may succeed after you!"

IF YOU SUFFER WITHOUT SUCCEEDING, IT IS THAT SOMEONE ELSE MAY SUCCEED AFTER YOU!

"I studied the life of Winston Churchill," my friend said. "He was one of the greatest leaders in history and had a reputation for never quitting and never complaining. Churchill's speech to the British Parliament is famous,

> 'Even though large tracts of Europe and many old and famous States have fallen or may fall into the grip of the Gestapo and all the odious apparatus of Nazi rule, we shall not flag or fail. We shall go on to the end, we shall fight in France, we shall fight on the seas and oceans, we shall fight with growing confidence and growing strength in the air, we shall defend our Island, whatever the cost may be, we shall fight on the beaches, we shall fight on the landing grounds, we shall fight in the fields and in the streets, we shall fight in the hills; we shall never surrender, and even if, which I do

not for a moment believe, this Island or a large part of it were subjugated and starving, then our Empire beyond the seas, armed and guarded by the British Fleet, would carry on the struggle, until, in God's good time, the New World, with all its power and might, steps forth to the rescue and the liberation of the old.'"

"Dan, talk about a no excuse zone, Churchill was a walking, talking no excuse zone."

My friend went on to tell me that we all face times of wanting to quit when things are hard or our backs are against the wall. He then explained about John Wesley, one of the greatest preachers and most effective communicators of his era.

Wesley was once denied a pulpit of a particular church so he went to the cemetery and used his father's head stone as his pulpit to passionately proclaim the truths of salvation to the people.

He told me of another great preacher, George Whitefield, who returned home from an extensive preaching tour and folks gathered outside his door at home. Instead of resting, he invited them in and he preached by candle light from the stairs. He died that night in his sleep. He too had set up a no excuse zone for his life.

The key to keeping life simple, and to win at anything in life, is to stay in the game even if you're ignored, denied or exhausted. Simply stop making excuses!

There are four types of people when it comes to excuses: The Should'a; Would'a; Could'a; or Did it! I love the anonymous quote: "Excuses are the tools of incompetence, used to build monuments of nothingness."

I love decisive people. I love it when I meet people that know what they're supposed to do with their lives. Decisive people stand out in a crowd. I saw a poster on the Internet one day. It said: "Roses are red, violets are blue, go to the gym!" Tyrese Gibson said, "Excuses sound best to the one that is making 'em up!"

If we're going to make our lives a "No Excuse Zone" then our motto ought to read something like this: "Every pro was once an amateur, every expert was once a beginner, so dream big and start now!" Every great finish had a start, and every start begins with a decision. Our decisions are shaped by several things: they are shaped by our environment, by the person who raised you, how you were raised, and those who were closest to you. Were your closest influencers optimistic, positive, godly people? Or were your influencers pessimistic negative and spiritually unengaged people? If your role models were the latter then you have some serious work to do! The environment of your mind can and must be developed so excuses aren't an option. To illustrate just how important our environment is to how we value ourselves and other things, I want to share a story:

Many years ago an antique motorcycle enthusiast was at a garage sale in Tennessee. As he's looking around the garage he saw an old motorcycle laying against the back wall. He thought he knew what it was but snapped a few pictures of the old broken down motorcycle. He texted the pictures to his friend who was an avid collector. He asked his friend to check a few things on the bike and send to send him a few more pictures. Once the man had sent the additional pictures, his friend told him to buy the bike for whatever the guy wanted for it. The man with the garage sale was asking $10,000 for the bike. He bought it and called his friend he just paid $10,000 for the motorcycle. The man immediately bought the motorcycle from him for $100,000. Once he had the old beat up motorcycle shipped to him, he lifted the seat of the old Harley Davidson and there was a plaque attached to the under side of the seat. It was dated and the plaque read: "Made for the King, Elvis Presley." The man restored the motorcycle and sold it to a famous late night T.V. host for a whopping $500,000. Why was this old bike so valuable? Because of who it previously belonged to. Because Elvis owned it, the value increased exponentially. We have to start thinking differently about ourselves because we belong to the King of Kings! He sought us, He bought us, and He lives in us. You are very, very valuable.

Our influencers shaped us and made us in obvious and subtle ways. Our life experiences and repetitious information we are exposed to also affect and shape our belief system. Habits, experiences, mentors all have tremendous impact on our decisions. The great news is if we've been raised in less than favorable circumstances, we can effect change in our mind, our will and our emotions. The brain is a muscle in a sense that it can be developed or neglected. Failure to renew your mind and develop your soul will lead to frustration and the status quo will be the best you can hope for. But that's for the other guys, not us! The path of least resistance is always the path of least results. It's a lot of work to travel uphill. Overcoming passive, negative thinking will be work but it's worth it. A symptom of a negative mindset is that you'll start judging those who are working to succeed, and make excuses why you can't do the same. You'll scale back your expectation and your goals will shrink to a new low. We can correct flawed thinking like a lack, poverty, insecure mindset by getting right information, implementing repetition according to Proverbs 20:5: *"Counsel in the heart of man is like deep water, but a man of understanding will draw it out."*

Let's re-visit some famous excuse makers:

- Moses told God he couldn't speak. *"Then Moses said to the Lord, 'O my Lord, I am not eloquent, neither before nor since You have spoken to Your servant; but I am slow of speech and slow of tongue.'"* —Exodus 4:10
- Esther thought she didn't have the right to approach the King. *"Then Esther spoke to Hathach, and gave him a command for Mordecai: 'All the king's servants and the people of the king's provinces know that any man or woman who goes into the inner court to the king, who has not been called, he has but one*

law: put all to death, except the one to whom the king holds out the golden scepter, that he may live. Yet I myself have not been called to go in to the king these thirty days.'" —Esther 4:1011

- The lame man said he couldn't get into the water when it was troubled. *"When Jesus saw him lying there, and knew that he already had been in that condition a long time, He said to him, 'Do you want to be made well?' The sick man answered Him, 'Sir, I have no man to put me into the pool when the water is stirred up; but while I am coming, another steps down before me.'"* —John 5:6-7

- Ten of the twelve spies said they were not able to go against the people. *"Then they told him, and said: 'We went to the land where you sent us. It truly flows with milk and honey, and this is its fruit. Nevertheless the people who dwell in the land are strong; the cities are fortified and very large; moreover we saw the descendants of Anak there. The Amalekites dwell in the land of the South; the Hittites, the Jebusites, and the Amorites dwell in the mountains; and the Canaanites dwell by the sea and along the banks of the Jordan.'"* —Numbers 13:27-29

- Adam and Eve blamed the serpent for their disobedience. *"And the Lord God said to the woman, 'What is this you have done?' The woman said, 'The serpent deceived me, and I ate.'"* —Genesis 3:13

- The people and leadership we're divided. *"So Ahab sent for all the children of Israel, and gathered the prophets together on Mount Carmel. And Elijah came to all the people, and said, 'How long will you falter between two opinions? If the Lord is God, follow Him; but if Baal, follow him.' But the people answered him not a word."* —1 Kings 18:20-21

Excuses will get in the way, especially when God wants to promote you, since He is going to give you an instruction that must be obeyed. Obey even if you're afraid.

"Do not harden your hearts, as in the rebellion, in the day of trial in the wilderness, when your fathers tested Me; They tried Me, though they saw My work. For forty years I was grieved with that generation, and said, 'It is a people who go astray in their hearts, And they do not know My ways.'"

—Psalm 95:8-10

That is because God is a faith God and we respond by faith, action and obedience.

GOD IS A FAITH GOD AND WE RESPOND BY FAITH, ACTION AND OBEDIENCE!

"So Samuel said: 'Has the Lord as great delight in burnt offerings and sacrifices, as in obeying the voice of the Lord? Behold, to obey is better than sacrifice, and to heed than the fat of rams.'" —1 Samuel 15:22

If we are going to keep it simple, then our lives must be no excuse zones. Excuses are like arm pits. We all have a couple and sometimes they stink. I know a family that had several children. They were always finding stray dogs and cats and bringing them home. The father of the family looked at all those strays and always took them to the pound because he didn't want to be bothered or have to raise them himself. One day, a few of the boys found a beautiful Brittany Spaniel. Even a blind man could see it was a special dog and the father put an ad in the paper. In In several weeks,, the owner of the dog spotted the ad and was able to come over and collect his prized pet. The dog was a three-time blue ribbon winner in his class.

The dog was very rare and the man was so grateful to get his prize pet back that he offered to give a puppy to the family from its next liter as a thank you. Although the children were crushed after having the dog for a couple of months, they finally were given the promised puppy months later. Unfortunately, the father wanted his now champion dog to be a working hunting dog rather than merely a family pet and he began to train it with no experience in doing so.

It only took one generation to go from champion blue ribbon winner to a dog that was fearful, cowering and not house broken. The father would drag the dog around, yell at it, hit it and keep it caged. After only one month, the dog would not respond to the father beyond cowering and shaking. The father relinquished the dog to the children while blaming them for the dog's lack of progress in becoming a champion hunting dog.

After interviewing the family, I learned that some of the children experienced bed wetting well past the usual age of control and some were also thumb suckers.

Further investigation proved that they too were fearful of the father. In fact, the children still talk about the callousness of their father years later.

In one generation the dog went from champion to nothing more than a whimpering shaking heel hound. The same can be said of the children. Several turned to alcohol and drugs to adapt to the fears they felt being brought up by their father. All of them left home as soon as they graduated high school or quit school, just to get out of the house. Some of them are still trying to adjust and a few are simply stuck in neutral.

A lesson to be learned here about child rearing and dog training is simply that a little affection and attention goes a long way. Also, playing the blame game as the father did with children was just an excuse for his own failure. It was Benjamin Franklin who said, "He that is good for making excuses is seldom good for anything else." Excuses are for the other guy not you.

My friend also taught me that day never to tell people your problems! Wow, I said to him, never? He said unless they're a trusted friend that you know will give you sound wisdom to get out of your problem don't tell them. He said 90 % of people don't care that you have troubles and 10% are glad you have them.

Excuses come in many different sizes and shapes. If we're not careful, we can be like Moses and think we are much too small to do the job or think the job is too small to be done (Exodus 3:7-10). But we see how Moses' self-centeredness took over in Verse 11 when he used the pronoun I twice as he tried to marginalize himself in God's plan.

"But Moses said to God, 'Who am I that I should go to Pharaoh, and that I should bring the children of Israel out of Egypt?'" —Exodus 3:11

Yet, God's awesomeness always comes through as He gives us instructions. Moses factored too much (I) into the equation and God had to remind him that the Big (I) would be with him.

"So He said, 'I will certainly be with you. And this shall be a sign to you that I have sent you: When you have brought the people out of Egypt, you shall serve God on this mountain.'" —Exodus 3:12

For you it may be the opposite and you think the job is too big or you're not big enough for the job. We have all felt that way at one time or another. That is why God calls us to do things that are too big for us so it will take faith.

There is a great story we can all relate to in 1 Kings 17 which shows how God leads us to do something that can be either beyond us or doesn't make sense to our minds and, if we're not diligent, the excuse game can begin.

"And Elijah the Tishbite, of the inhabitants of Gilead, said to Ahab, 'As the Lord God of Israel lives, before whom I stand, there shall not be dew nor rain these years, except at my word.' Then the word of the Lord came to him, saying, 'Get away from here and turn eastward, and hide by the Brook

Cherith, which flows into the Jordan. And it will be that you shall drink from the brook, and I have commanded the ravens to feed you there."' —1 Kings 17:1-4

God told the prophet Elijah to speak to King Ahab and tell him that the rain was going to stop because this ungodly king had tolerated Baal as their focus of worship. Baal was the god of rain. God's way of answering this king's actions was to send a powerful prophet with power in his words and confidence in his God. Once Elijah speaks and commands the rains to cease, God leads him to the brook Cherith where he will drink water and the ravens would bring him food.

These seem like crazy instructions to say the least since there is not a man alive who would want to eat from scraps brought by a traditionally dirty bird known as a scavenger. Yet we see that Elijah obeyed God and God provided for him until the drought even dried up the brook Cherith.

"So he went and did according to the word of the Lord, for he went and stayed by the Brook Cherith, which flows into the Jordan. The ravens brought him bread and meat in the morning, and bread and meat in the evening; and he drank from the brook. And it happened after a while that the brook dried up, because there had been no rain in the land." —1 Kings 17:5-7

Then God spoke to the prophet again and told him that it was time to move. This time it makes even less sense than the brook and the birds.

"Then the word of the Lord came to him, saying, 'Arise, go to Zarephath, which belongs to Sidon, and dwell there. See, I have commanded a widow there to provide for you."' —Kings 17:8-9

So, God tells the prophet that even in the middle of a drought and even with a single mother, I can meet all of your and her needs.

This is head scratching to say the least. The next thing here is you don't see any push back from Elijah. I don't know what Elijah was thinking but spam and oatmeal was probably all he could expect from a widow in a drought if she was doing well. What if she's broke and has nothing? I guarantee you the last thing the prophet wanted to do was be a burden to a widow.

One of the most humbling things you'll ever do is receive offerings from people who you know are in need. But I also know our giving is our very lifeline to favor and the prosperity that is in our future.

"Give, and it will be given to you: good measure, pressed down, shaken together, and running over will be put into your bosom. For with the same measure that you use, it will be measured back to you." —Luke 6:38

"For you know the grace of our Lord Jesus Christ, that though He was rich, yet for your sakes He became poor, that you through His poverty might become rich." —2 Corinthians 8:9

Again, no push back from Elijah the prophet. He hasn't used any of the typical excuses you might hear from some folk. He didn't ask what most of us were thinking. You know the, 'I'll go if you really want me to but please not to a widow woman who has a son during a drought. I didn't say anything at the brook and I never complained about the ravens delivering my meals but come on, a widow, Lord?' No, he didn't say any of that.

"So he arose and went to Zarephath. And when he came to the gate of the city, indeed a widow was there gathering sticks. And he called to her and said, 'Please bring me a little water in a cup, that I may drink.'" —1 Kings 17:10

As Elijah went to Zarephath we can only imagine what was going through his head. I could list at least ten off the top of mine. I know one thing for sure, he never questioned God's wisdom or

God's plan. Once he got to the gate of the city, there was that widow woman gathering sticks.

I can see Elijah shaking his head and smiling as he got to the city gate. Once he spotted her, he probably got excited to see how God would supply the rest of his needs. This is dynamic in its simplicity as he asks her for a drink in the middle of a drought. He simply asks, 'a little water in a cup that I may drink.' To you and I that may seem like a low level commitment, but remember, she is as desperate as a single mom who is a widow could be. This speaks volumes of her character to do what she did, even when she had such obvious needs.

"And as she was going to get it, he called to her and said, 'Please bring me a morsel of bread in your hand.'"
—1 Kings 17:11

In my mind, this is the kicker. It's just like God, once He gets us moving, He always pushes us beyond our original expectation.

When I first got saved, I wanted to serve God. I was already out in the business world but I wanted whatever gifts I had to glorify God to the max, so I prayed a very scary prayer. "Lord, use me. I want to serve you. Just don't make me work with folks who have addictions, amen." In retrospect, I think God must have heard and thought, "So Dan, you'll serve me doing whatever, except working with people with drug problems. Is that about it?"

Within a year, I was working in Manhattan, preaching the Gospel and helping heroin addicts get into drug rehabilitation centers. I was making excuses and setting up parameters for God to use me. Pretty funny, isn't it? God does to us what Elijah did to the widow woman. Once he gets us moving, He challenges us to go beyond our original expectation.

Elijah asks for a little water and once she started to move in that direction, he also asks for a morsel of bread. For many, this would be a convenient spot for an excuse. After all, the widow had no husband and had no bread made.

"So she said, 'As the Lord your God lives, I do not have bread, only a handful of flour in a bin, and a little oil in a jar; and see, I am gathering a couple of sticks that I may go in and prepare it for myself and my son, that we may eat it, and die.'"

—1 Kings 17:12

Her explanation certainly proves how desperate she is. I love how God gives her a word to act on.

"And Elijah said to her, 'Do not fear; go and do as you have said, but make me a small cake from it first, and bring it to me; and afterward make some for yourself and your son. For thus says the Lord God of Israel: "The bin of flour shall not be used up, nor shall the jar of oil run dry, until the day the Lord sends rain on the earth."'"   —1 Kings 17:13-14

He basically tells her not to fear. As a side note, there are 365 fear nots in your Bible, one for each day of the year. The Bible teaches that in the last days there will be perilous times. Many believe the time is now as they watch TV and hear the news about famines, droughts, storms, Christians being persecuted and killed for their faith and terrorism around the world.

So, God has this desperate woman with no options but to eat and die, give the first bite to the prophet. As far as we can see, she didn't blink or resist. She kept it simple by not over reasoning spiritual issues to the point that she found an excuse not to obey. That is a great example for us!

God has promised He will meet our needs and even prosper us.

"And my God shall supply all your need according to His riches in glory by Christ Jesus."   —Philippians 4:19

When the pressures are on, the question is do we obey or do we find an excuse?

I've learned from experience that radical obedience brings radical blessings.

RADICAL OBEDIENCE BRINGS RADICAL BLESSINGS!

Whatever your need, God has the ability to meet you right where you are. You can get pretty bold when you know God stands by all His promises.

"For all the promises of God in Him are Yes, and in Him Amen, to the glory of God through us." —2 Corinthians 1:20

"Now this is the confidence that we have in Him, that if we ask anything according to His will, He hears us. And if we know that He hears us, whatever we ask, we know that we have the petitions that we have asked of Him."
—1 John 5:14-15

"If you ask anything in My name, I will do it." —John 14:14

Excuses are for people who don't serve God or they don't know God. It is impossible for God to lie.

"God is not a man, that He should lie, Nor a son of man, that He should repent. Has He said, and will He not do? Or has He spoken, and will He not make it good?" —Numbers 23:19

You and I can be as down and out as the widow woman, or we can be an up and outer, which is simply people who have everything financially but are bankrupt spiritually and emotionally.

We are believers and not excuse makers. We choose to serve and trust God with our lives and futures. We choose to live in a no excuse zone.

There is a poem by Mayme White Miller that sums up what my new friend was trying to get across to me entitled "Yourself To Blame."

If things go bad for you
And make you a bit ashamed
Often you will find out that
You have yourself to blame
Swiftly we ran to mischief
And then the bad luck came
Why do we fault others?
We have ourselves to blame
Whatever happens to us,
Here is what we say
"Had it not been for so-and-so
Things wouldn't have gone that way."
And if you are short of friends,
I'll tell you what to do
Make an examination,
You'll find the fault's in you...
You're the captain of your ship,
So agree with the same
If you travel downward
You have yourself to blame

It has been said that you are not a failure until you start blaming others.

* *

THE KEEP IT SIMPLE MENTALITY IS BEING
A NO EXCUSE ZONE!

IN CONCLUSION

I have read and reread the legal size page front and back filled with scripture, quotes and quips many times over the years. My friend passed away several years ago but I've got a little piece of his wisdom here with me in my study to reflect and glean from.

We all have many people come in and out of our lives over the years. With some you learn what to do and with others you learn what not to do.

Keeping it simple and not letting your start stop you is about proactive learning and managing the unknown, the kind of education that you get from learning from your mistakes and the success of others. We all must go through the university of adversity and the school of hard knocks. I'll never forget my friend and I have been fortunate to visit with his son from time to time over the years since he's passed. It is truly a blessing to see my friend's wisdom living on in his son.

It is important to remember those that say they can and those that say they can't are both right. So wherever you are in your life, you must start to change those things that are hindering you and begin a journey into your future. Don't wait for inspiration or a sign, start where you are and the sooner the better. Don't fall for the excuse "I waiting on the Lord" because more times than not He's the one that's waiting on you. If you're looking for an excuse any old one will do.

Don't do what unsuccessful people do. Decide today to break out of old patterns and download new ways of thinking into your soul. When you make a mistake, brush yourself off and start over where you left off before the detour. There is nothing new you can learn from hitting your thumb with a hammer a second time.

Ask God to give you a discerning eye to see what others are missing. Ask Him to help you see the diamonds others are stepping over. Remember, there is gold out there and someone is going to find it. The one who looks for it diligently is the one who gets it.

* * * *

THERE IS GOLD OUT THERE AND THE ONE WHO LOOKS FOR IT IS THE ONE WHO GETS IT!

* * * *

Focus on the important and not just the immediate. Light dispersed can brighten up an entire room but light focused like a laser can cut steel like butter. Your focus can bring you favor, prosperity, opportunity and progress. When you're focused it's amazing how the right people enter into your world.

Stay humble because, if you don't, the people you pass on the way up will still be there when you are on the way down. You see, God is not mocked, whatever you sow...you reap.

"Do not be deceived, God is not mocked; for whatever a man sows, that he will also reap." —Galatians 6:7

Somebody up there likes you so keep your eyes on Him and trust in Him. Nothing can separate you from the love of God.

Remember, everyone is leading someone. Although we all may not have a large platform who cares? Just be faithful where you are and lead yourself, your family and your finances into a bright future.

Excuses are for the other guy not us. You and God make the majority and nothing, and I mean nothing, is too difficult for Him.

If you're on your way to heaven, make it one of your life's goals not to arrive alone. Be a light in the darkness and be salt on the earth.

In penning this book, I only got part way through the legal paper that my friend gave me. He has so many more truths that transform, I could go on and on and probably sometime in the future I will.

* *

FROM FORT MYERS FLORIDA,
KEEP IT SIMPLE!

ABOUT THE AUTHOR

Daniel J. Haight is Senior Pastor and founder of Celebration Family Church for over 25 years in beautiful Fort Myers, FL. Together with his wife Joselyn, they have 4 children and 4 grandchildren. Daniel Haight has authored *Faith That Takes*, and *Keys To Maximizing Your Harvest*. He is a prolific writer, and conference speaker. He has a thoughtful and humorous approach to his seminars that is captivating and informative. He has traveled to Europe, Africa and throughout the Caribbean speaking at churches, in conferences and seminars. Daniel Haight has hosted a local television and radio program called the "Force of Faith" broadcast. He has also developed an App called "7x7 Revolution" to encourage believers to stop 7 times a day and acknowledge God. This App is available at both the Apple App Store and Google Play.

Follow Pastor Daniel on Facebook @Daniel J. Haight, on Twitter @ pastordjh and Instagram @Daniel J. Haight.